VISUAL GUIDE :: COLLE(

Casa Batlló

PHOTOGRAPHS: CARLOS GIORDANO AND NICOLÁS PALMISANO

DOSDEARTE EDICIONES

01

contents

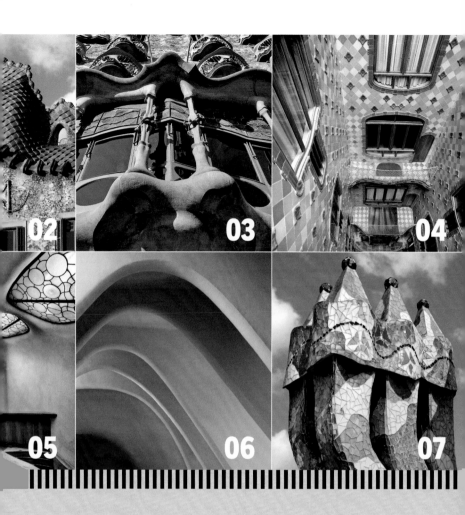

01

The origins of Casa Batlló

Barcelona makes the most of its industrial potential

At heady speed towards a modern, industrialized society, Barcelona expands and metamorphoses. In the year 1888, it plays host to the first Universal Exhibition of Spain, ranking it as one of the most important cities in Europe. It is a period of intense cultural activity accompanied by a revival of Catalan values and within this context will soon appear one of Antoni Gaudí's masterpieces: Casa Batlló.

A period of change

In the latter part of the 19th century, Catalonia underwent a great cultural revival, reflected, above all, in its literature, music, plastic arts and architecture. This movement, called the *Renaixença*, advocated, amongst other things, the use of the Catalan language, which had been confined to the privacy of the home. The revivification of these values, teamed with Barcelona's industrial growth, encouraged a nationalist fervour that echoed throughout all fields.

Can Batlló industrial estate

CHRONOLOGY
KEY FACTS ABOUT GAUDÍ'S PERIOD

1851
First Universal Exhibition
London hosts the first exhibition in Crystal Palace.

1859
Oil exploration
Edwin Drake is said to be the discoverer of *"liquid gold"*.

1867
The first volume of the book *The Capital*. It was in this essay that Karl Marx dissected the capitalist system.

1870
The Third French Republic. King Louis Napoleon III abdicated after France's defeat in the war against Prussia.

Columbus pointing at America

Monument to Christopher Columbus
Constructed by Gaietà Buigas i Monravà for the Universal Exhibition of 1888, it stands at the end of the Ramblas.

A *Universal* city

Barcelona played host to the first Universal Exhibition of Spain in the year 1888, endeavouring to promote the country as an industrial force and therefore extend trade beyond its borders. The Town Hall subsequently carried out numerous urban developments that would turn Barcelona into a thriving European metropolis.

1888

THE CIUTADE-LLA PARK
was inaugurated, where the first Universal Exhibition of Barcelona took place.

◦ **Barcelona towards the end of the 19th century**

A daring and avant-garde bourgeoisie

While the rest of Spain was still largely agricultural, a sound, industrial framework was being established in Catalonia, with Barcelona city at the helm, making it the Spanish region that most quickly incorporated the changes provoked by the Industrial Revolution. This economic prosperity led to the rise of a flourishing, industrialist bourgeoisie that would become promoter, whether as client or patron, of numerous artistic and architectonic projects.

NOTE
TEXTILE INDUSTRY IN CATALONIA

The textile industry was pioneering in its use of steam machinery.

Textile mills	Manual	Mechanical
1841	24.880	231
1850	24.008	5.580
1861	12.026	9.695

1874
Cezanne sells his first painting *Maison de Pendu*. The artist was unknown in his time.

1876
Invention of the telephone
This marvel has changed people's way of communicating.

1879
Edison invents the electric bulb
This invention led to the generalization of electrical illumination.

Casa Batlló on Passeig de Gràcia

Barcelona's most emblematic avenue comes about

Due to the city's significant growth in population, the urban development plan for the Eixample is devised, linking the old nucleus of the city with the municipalities on the outskirts. Passeig de Gràcia emerges and soon becomes the city's main thoroughfare, selected by the Catalan bourgeoisie to raise stunning architectonic works. It is here that Antoni Gaudí builds Casa Batlló.

The Eixample

At the beginning of the 19th century Barcelona experienced an unprecedented growth in population. Its flourishing industry drew thousands of labourers and the city, surrounded by an ancient wall, could no longer hold all of its inhabitants. The sanitary situation was abysmal and the cholera epidemic in 1854 hastened the decision to do away with the city walls. The demolishment made way for the Eixample, an urban development project conceived by an engineer called Cerdà and which was approved in 1859. It consisted of a huge grid of perpendicular and parallel streets, whose blocks had cut off angles, forming chamfered corners to aid visibility, with construction solely permitted on two sides of the block with the remainder devoted to garden areas.

The fashionable avenue. At the beginning of the 20th century, Passeig de Gràcia was the city's most prestigious avenue. Barcelonans would go strolling down the boulevard, perusing the windows of its luxury shops or frequenting the theatre.

1905

IS WHEN
Passeig de Gràcia's installations are improved, when lamps are fitted and the street is paved.

○ **Passeig de Gràcia at the start of the 20th century**

CHRONOLOGY
KEY FACTS ABOUT GAUDÍ'S PERIOD

1883
The motorcycle arrives. The German engineer Gottlieb Daimler creates the first motorcycle.

1886
The automobile arrives. In January, Karl Benz applies to the German government for a patent for a three-wheeled vehicle.

1889
The Eiffel Tower is inaugurated
It was erected for the Universal Exhibition of Paris of 1889.

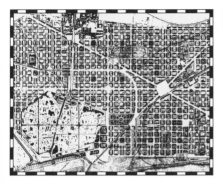

The Eixample
Barcelona's urban development project was devised in such a way that every zone had all services: schools, hospitals, markets and so on. These changes would make it a fairer and more equitable city.

Ildefons Cerdà, the Eixample's creator
The town planner devised an egalitarian city to be enjoyed by all.

Passeig de Gràcia

The city's most important thoroughfare was, in the past, the shortest route between the city of Barcelona and the town of Gràcia, a small locality situated three kilometres away. The fountains, gardens and recreational areas on either side of the avenue lured the Barcelonans and with the expansion of the city, the avenue soon became the Eixample's spinal cord. In 1905, now illuminated and paved, the main forms of transport started circulating and the avenue was chosen by the wealthiest of figures to construct their homes on, which were then designed by prestigious architects. The Batlló family decided, within this context, to entrust their house to an ingenious architect: Antoni Gaudí.

Passeig de Gràcia today
At present, the avenue's elegance and architectonic splendour still remain intact.

Casa Batlló and Casa Amatller

1894
Invention of the radio. The Italian Marconi was the first person that managed to send radio signals.

1895
First cinema projection
It took place in Paris, organized by the Lumière brothers.

1897
Aspirin
It was created by the German chemist, Félix Hoffman, after numerous experiments.

1898
Independence of Cuba
The Spanish war against the United States led to the loss of Cuba.

The promoter, Josep Batlló

The textile industrialist entrusts his house to Gaudí

Josep Batlló and his wife, Amalia Godó, purchased a modest building on Passeig de Gràcia with the intention of living with their family in the new Eixample, a fashionable and prestigious area. In his eagerness to stand out from the crowd, Josep set out to build a spectacular house and to carry out the project, he contracted the services of one of the most innovative architects of the period, the ingenious Antoni Gaudí.

The Batlló family

Josep Batlló i Casanovas was a businessman from a distinguished family, dedicated to the textile industry that owned various factories in Barcelona. In 1884, he married Amalia Godó and they went on to have five offspring. On the 30th of December of 1903, they chose to reside in the Eixample and bought a simple building on 43, Passeig de Gràcia for the sum of 510,000 pesetas (3.072 euros), planning to demolish it and replace it with an imposing house.

Josep Batlló
The promoter wanted his house to be the most striking on Passeig de Gràcia, which was the most important avenue of the time.

1903
IS THE YEAR
in which the textile industrialist buys the property with the intention of building a family house, which Antoni Gaudí duly carried out.

Casa Enric Batlló, Josep's brother

1901
Van Gogh exhibition in Paris
His artistic genius was recognised eleven years after his death.

1902
Alfonso XIII King of Spain
At the age of 16 he took on his duties as Head of State.

1903
First piloted flight
The brothers Wilbur and Orville Wright invented the first motorised aeroplane.

The block of discord. In the same block on Passeig de Gràcia, Puig i Cadafalch built Casa Amatller; Domènech i Montaner built Casa Lleó Morera and Gaudí finished the renovation of Casa Batlló.

The period of Modernism

From the end of the 19th century to the start of the 20th century, the rupture with the past, the search for a new style and the desire for modernity stretched across the arts. At its maximum expression, architecture knew how to integrate traditional crafts such as ceramic work, wrought iron work, stained glass windows and sculpture, generating magnificent works of art corresponding to the ideals of modernist beauty. Modernism transformed the city of Barcelona. Within this context, Antoni Gaudí stood out from the architects of the period and in his relentless search for new architectonic solutions he generated an expressive and personal style, his work drawing from modernist ideals and inspiring new artistic trends.

Domènech i Montaner
He was one of the most important and well-known architects of Modernism.

Puig i Cadafalch
His work combines Gothic-Catalan elements with Nordic influence.

1905
Einstein announces the theory of relativity. The German scientist revolutionized the classical concepts of physics.

1911
Machu Pichu is rediscovered
The North American, Hiram Bingham, discovers the Inca ruins.

1912
The Titanic sinks
On the night of the 14th of April, on its maiden voyage, the great ocean liner goes down.

1913
Rite of Spring
Russian composer Igor Stravinski presents this famous ballet.

An architect with fresh ideas

Gaudí designs Casa Batlló while eschewing out-dated concepts

Fascinated by Gaudí, the textile industrialist, Josep Batlló, commissioned the architect with the construction of his house. It was 1904 and the 52-year-old genius was in his professional prime. Mature personally as well as artistically, Gaudí was ready to undertake a unique and fresh project and the complete renovation of an old building situated on Passeig de Gràcia would immediately convert into a universal work of art.

The commission

At a time when the bourgeoisie counted on the services of a personal architect, the Batlló clan had the well-known architect Josep Vilaseca, but Josep Batlló was in pursuit of something different for his new abode. Through the Llimona brothers, he meets Gaudí, and awestruck by the architect's innovative ideas, immediately commissions him with a project: a house where his family will occupy the main floor and the rest of the residences are rented out, common practice amongst the bourgeoisie of the period. Gaudí's commission was to demolish the old building and construct a new one, but he managed to persuade the promoter to carry out just renovation work and in November of 1904 planning permission was applied for.

52
YEARS OLD
was Gaudí age when he accepted the commission of the renovation work on Casa Batlló, which started in 1904 and ended in 1906.

Antoni Gaudí
The architect was working on the Sagrada Familia, Park Güell and the Torre Bellesguard when he embarked on the renovation of the Casa Batlló.

CHRONOLOGY
KEY FACTS ABOUT GAUDÍ'S PERIOD

1914
World War I
Known as the Great War, involving 32 countries.

1916
Birth of Dadaism
This artistic movement surged as a criticism of western culture.

DADA
DADA
DADA
was ist DADA?
☞ Philosophie?
Religion?

1917
The Russian Revolution
After overthrowing the Tsar, Russia became a Soviet state.

The third work on the avenue
Casa Batlló was the third work on Passeig de Gràcia. The Gibert pharmacy (1879) and the Bar Torino (1902) preceded it.

The life of Antoni Gaudí

1852
He is born on the 25th of June in Reus.

1868
He moves to Barcelona to study architecture.

1875
He does military service.

1876
He collaborates with the architect Josep Fontserè on the Ciutadella Park. His brother and mother die.

1878
He finishes his architecture studies and designs lamp posts for the Plaça Reial and Pla del Palau. He projects the Workers' Cooperative of Mataro. He exhibits in the Universal Exhibition of Paris of 1878.

1883
Work on the Caprice starts, in Comillas, and ends in 1885. He begins work on Casa Vincens, which he finishes in 1888. He takes control of the work on Sagrada Familia.

1889
He constructs the Episcopal Palace of Astorga and Casa de los Botines.

1900
Casa Calvet is awarded prize for best building by the City Council. Work on Park Güell starts.

1904
He is commissioned to renovate Casa Batlló.

1906
La Pedrera is started. He moves to Park Güell with his father and niece. His father dies at the age of 93.

1910
He receives a commission for a hotel in New York.

1911
Ill with Maltese fever he moves to Puigcerdà, where he draws up his will.

1912
His niece, Rosita, dies.

1914
Work is interrupted on Park Güell.

1918
His friend and patron, Eusebi Güell, dies.

1925
He moves into his study in Sagrada Familia.

1926
On the 7th of June a tram knocks him down. Three days later he dies at the age of 74.

A strict architect
Gaudí was not only known for his ingenious construction techniques but also for his exacting character, which led to a few heated moments with Josep Batlló. The architect never hesitated to change anything that did not coincide with his ideas, without taking the budget into account or planning permission. However, Mr. Batlló was captivated by the work and recommended the architect to his friend Pere Milà, who he would then build La Pedrera for.

1904
IS THE YEAR in which Gaudí is commissioned to design the Batlló family house.

La Pedrera
At this time, Gaudí's was greatly in demand and his services were required by wealthy characters such as the Milà family who entrusted their house to him.

Pinnacle on the Sagrada Familia

1917
First jazz record. The Original Dixieland Jazz Band produced the first album in history.

1918
The Great War ends. German surrender brought the war to an end with almost 10 million deaths.

1922
Tutankhamen A British man, Howard Carter, discovers the Egyptian pharaoh's tomb.

1926
The Sun Also Rises The writer Ernest Hemingway publishes this novel, which is deemed to be his first important work.

GAUDÍ'S MOST IMPORTANT WORKS

Universal and innovative, architect Antoni Gaudí left behind an architectonic legacy that still captivates today for its utter originality.

The architect
A genius and unclassifiable, Gaudí managed to generate his own unmistakeable style in his work.

CHRONOLOGY OF THE WORKS

1883	1885	1887	1889	1891	1893	1895	1897

2
3
4
5
6
7
8
9

01

Temple of the Sagrada Familia
Considered as Gaudí's most outstanding work, it is the synthesis of all his architecture.

02

Casa Vicens
It was the first house that Antoni Gaudí completely designed.

04

Finca Güell
Located in Barcelona, it was the first commission from Eusebi Güell, who would later be his patron.

05

Palau Güell. Situated in the heart of Barcelona, it is a work of great sobriety.

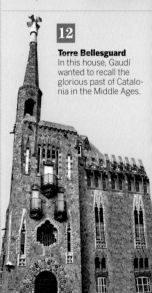

12

Torre Bellesguard
In this house, Gaudí wanted to recall the glorious past of Catalonia in the Middle Ages.

06

Teresian College. He plans the lecture rooms for the college situated in Barcelona.

 11

Park Güell
Constructed between 1900 and 1914, it was devised as a garden city project. In the year 1984, UNESCO declared the park a World Heritage Site.

1899	1901	1903	1905	1907	1909	1911	1913	1915	1926

1
11
12
13
 14

13

Casa Batlló
This building is an exceptional example of Gaudí's organic architecture. On its façade, the balconies appear to hang like carnival masks.

14

La Pedrera
On finishing the colourful Casa Batlló, Gaudí was commissioned with the building of another dwelling on Passeig de Gràcia, the Milà's house. Built between 1906 and 1912, it is yet another masterpiece by this outstanding architect.

07

Episcopal palace
Gaudí designed the residence of the Bishop of Astorga (León) in line with the Gothic style.

03

The Caprice
When designing this residence, Gaudí blended the style of the Middle Ages with the ostentation of oriental palaces.

08

Casa de los Botines
It is located in the historic centre of León.

10

Casa Calvet
Refined and sober, it received prize for best building of 1900 from the City Council.

09

The Güell wine cellars
They were built in the locality of Garraf.

02

GAUDÍ'S PROJECT

A burst of enthusiasm

Gaudí, at his most creative, turns the simple renovation of a house into a universal work of art.

Antoni Gaudí's creative force can be appreciated in each one of his works, but it is especially apparent in Casa Batlló where he draws on all his imagination and ingenuity. It was in 1904 when the industrialist Josep Batlló commissioned Gaudí with the renovation of a house that he had purchased the year before. Situated on Passeig de Gràcia, the most important avenue of the period, the house was constructed between 1904 and 1906 and is, in fact, a radical alteration of a sober Eixample building that was constructed around 1877. The architect, having reached artistic maturity and unshackled by academician influences, saw this project as a way of unleashing all his artistic creativity. Gaudí was already a respected architect, but the location of the house, in *the block of discord*, meant he would be sharing space with the best architects of the era. Maybe influenced by this fact or by his innate genius, the architect designed a house where a feeling of gaiety exuded from each of its corners and where strict constructive functionalism could be blended with his intricate knowledge of the laws of nature. Although Casa Batlló is admired throughout the entire world, it wasn't until 2005, ninety-nine years after having been completed, that it was officially recognised as a work of art and declared a World Heritage Site by UNESCO.

Antoni Gaudí around 1915

The Casa Batlló

A unique work. Casa Batlló excited diverse interpretations by a society fascinated by the new. Gaudí's universe, controversial for its ingeniousness, completely unfurls in the block of discord.

An admired building

Detached from architectonic schools, Gaudí starts work on the house at the age of 52, when he was at the pinnacle of his creativity and artistic maturity. It was in this context that the architect transforms a sober building in the Barcelona Eixample into the marvellous Casa Batlló, which right from the start became an eulogy to happiness. Admired by citizens and architects alike, the house was nominated for the Barcelona City Council's prize for best building of 1906, but the jury awarded it to another architect, probably because Gaudí had already won it in the year 1900 for Casa Calvet.

Original work
Casa Batlló, Gaudí's most personal and original work, was selected, with six other projects, in the competition for the best building in Barcelona of 1906.

1904
WORK COMMENCES on the total renovation of the property purchased by Josep Batlló in 1903.

PASSEIG DE GRÀCIA FAÇADE

BALCONIES
They have a mask or skull-like shape.

ROSTRUM ON THE MAIN FLOOR

DOOR ENTRANCE
It leads into the general vestibule Gaudí designed, without edges and with curved forms.

CENTRAL PATIO WELL
It was designed to supply the house with adequate light and ventilation.

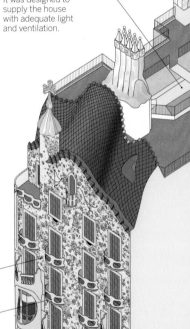

The façade. It looks like a choppy sea, like the drawings of Japanese artist Hokusai, who was in vogue at the time.

CHIMNEYS
Of organic shape and grouped together, they are topped with cowls decorated with *trencadís* work.

A sea of influences

As with all of Gaudí's works, the symbolic universe and resemblance to places and objects in nature were ever present in his undertakings and Casa Batlló was no exception to the rule. With curved shapes and of a char-acteristic cobalt blue colour, the Batlló family's property was clearly inspired by the ocean and in years to follow, these organic shapes created by Gaudí would influence new trends in modern art, such as in the case of Salvador Dalí.

REAR FAÇADE

THE BATLLÓ FAMILY'S TERRACE
Located above the ground floor, it is a private area that is accessed from the dining room.

The sea. The elements and spaces throughout the house evoke the marine-like universe typical of Gaudí.

A candy house
It has been likened to the house from the tale of Hansel and Gretel.

PARTITION WALL

1906
WORK FINISHES
on the complete renovation of Casa Batlló that had started two years before.

BASEMENT
It retains the cold-room of the farm-house that previously occupied this plot of land.

NOTE
PLANNING PERMISSION

Permission for renovation work on the house was applied for in 1904. Two years later, the Town Hall ordered that work be halted for not having the necessary authorization, though 2 weeks later, Mr. Batlló then told them that work was complete and then applied for permission to rent out the flats. The permit didn't arrive until 1913, though the tax fee due was even more delayed, unpaid until 1920.

An extraordinary building

An open and uninhibited space. Gaudí's *artistic freedom teamed with a boundless imagination, were never preferred to the principle of functionalism, whether on the exterior or interior of the house.*

Light and ventilation

One of the most important aspects of the project was the need for light in all areas, as during this period, interior rooms were generally dark. He therefore planned that the floor surround a large, central patio well that then transformed into the axis of the house because, as well as providing light and ventilation, it also linked the access ways and upward traffic with the neighbours' staircase and lift. By angling the rooms and bedrooms towards the street and the service areas towards the interior patio well, the architect was able to provide well-lit and ventilated rooms.

+4.300

METRES SQUARE
is the total surface area taken up by all the floors in Casa Batlló.

450

METRES SQUARE
is the area that each floor occupies, without counting the interior patio well.

14,50

METRES OF FAÇADE
is the total length of the house that Gaudí knew how to get the maximum out of.

9

BALCONIES
are distributed throughout the façade, two of them of different size and shape.

RESIDENCES
Each floor destined for renting is divided into two flats.

THE MAIN FLAT
The Batlló family's flat was here and took up the entire floor, measuring 450 metres square.

THE GROUND FLOOR
The area that had been initially planned as a car park was later used as a warehouse.

Main flat. Gaudí designed large windows looking out on to Passeig de Gràcia.

14,50 m

NOTE
ANTONI GAUDÍ'S COLLABORATORS

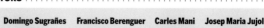

Passeig de Gràcia entrance

For the construction of Casa Batlló, Gaudí counted on the collaboration of a group of architects and artists that had worked alongside him on other projects.

Domingo Sugrañes   Francisco Berenguer   Carles Mani   Josep Maria Jujol

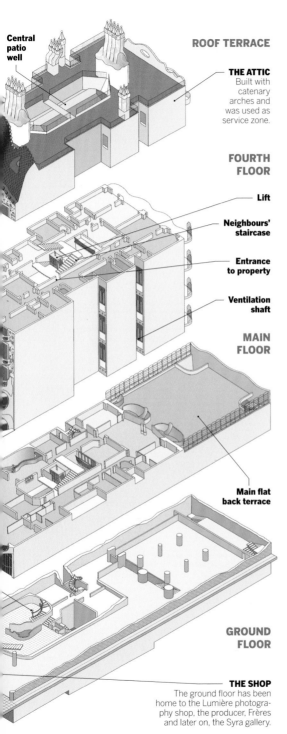

Central patio well

ROOF TERRACE

THE ATTIC
Built with catenary arches and was used as service zone.

FOURTH FLOOR

Lift

Neighbours' staircase

Entrance to property

Ventilation shaft

MAIN FLOOR

Main flat back terrace

GROUND FLOOR

THE SHOP
The ground floor has been home to the Lumière photography shop, the producer, Frères and later on, the Syra gallery.

The layout of the house

When renovating the house, Gaudí took into account how each space would carry out the function required by its inhabitants. This was how the basement was used as a coalbunker and held the lumber-rooms of the main apartment, the ground floor was used as the parking area, which was later turned into a warehouse, a shop and provided the neighbours with access to the staircase, the lift and the private vestibule of the Batlló family. The first floor would naturally be entirely taken up by the main apartment that the Batlló's would occupy and on the other floors there would be eight rented flats. Gaudí also topped the building with an attic that was used as a service area and he then covered the roof with a terrace.

Balconies. The organic and sinuous forms of Gaudí's work can be appreciated throughout the entire house.

THE BEFORE AND AFTER OF CASA BATLLÓ

Next to nothing remains of the former property built in 1877. The changes were radical and sweeping, using innovative techniques and without academic submissions.

Antoni Gaudí
Any work he projected would cause great expectation for its outstanding ingenuity and unexpected outcome.

THE ORIGINAL HOUSE
Built between 1875 and 1877 by architect and Gaudí's former teacher, Emilio Salas Cortés, the house clashed with its neighbours, which were much more fashionable. The property had a sober façade, a basement, ground floor, four floors, an interior mezzanine and garden at the rear. It wasn't at all interesting, except for its location.

3.100
METRES SQUARE
of constructed area was the size of the property acquired by Batlló for the sum of 510.000 pesetas in 1903.

21
METRES
was the height of the façade that was partially demolished in 1904, during Gaudí's renovation work.

THE BLOCK OF DISCORD
Gaudí constructed Casa Batlló, the highest edifice in the *manzana de la discordia*, without regard for the architectonic peculiarities of the neighbouring properties.

32 m
28 m
23 m

1   2   3   4   5   6

Four-armed cross

4.300
METRES SQUARE
of constructed
work is the total
area renovated by
Gaudí in less than
two years.

32
METRES
is the height
of Casa Batl-
ló's new and
spectacular
façade.

GAUDÍ'S RENOVATIONS
The architect carried out a complete
overhaul on the property. On the
outside, he transformed the main
façade by adding balconies and a
stone rostrum with original windows. Once inside, he altered the
entire main floor, enlarged the central patio and the basement, and
added two more floors where he put
an attic and the lumber rooms. All in
all, Gaudí converted a simple refur-
bishment into a work of art.

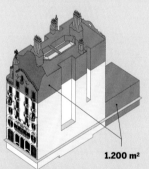

1.200 m²

Volume added by Gaudí
The Barcelona City Council wanted to
halt the work for the extra volume that
Gaudí added on to the former building.

1 **Casa Lleó Morera**
Passeig de Gràcia, 35
Year: 1902-1906
Architect:
Lluís Domènech i Montaner

2 **Casa Mulleras**
Passeig de Gràcia, 37
Year: 1906
Architect:
Enric Sagnier Villavecchia

3 **Casa Delfina Bonet**
Passeig de Gràcia, 39
Year: 1915
Architect:
Marcelí Coquillat Llofriu

4 **Casa Amatller**
Passeig de Gràcia, 41
Year: 1898-1900
Architect:
Josep Puig i Cadafalch

5 **Casa Batlló**
Passeig de Gràcia, 43
Year: 1904-1906
Architect:
Antoní Gaudí

6 **Casa Emilia Adrià**
Passeig de Gràcia, 45
Year: 1879
Architect:
Emilio Salas Cortés

01. The hall in 1927. The owner's property was accessed by a private staircase that started on the ground floor and went up to the hall. **02. Façade termination.** Its shape resembles an animal's spine. **03. The attic.** For this floor, Gaudí used catenary archways, a structural system different to the rest of the house. **04. Sculpted stone.** The rostrum on the main façade is made from stone sculpted with organic shapes. **05. The chimneys.** The roof terrace has 27 chimneys distributed into four groups. **06. The central patio well.** The architect widened the patio of the former house to obtain better illumination and ventilation for the apartments' interior rooms.

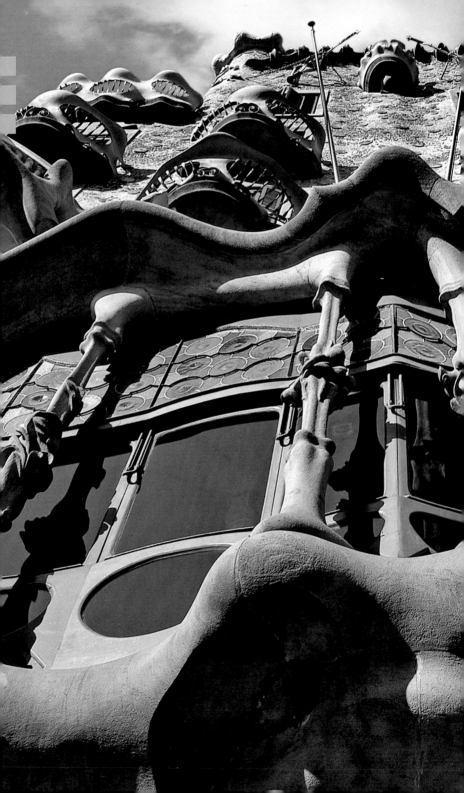

03

THE FAÇADE

Movement and colour

*Gaudí creates a vibrant and fantastical façade,
where curving shapes and colour abound.*

audí used all his genius when renovating Casa Batlló, but most of all on
the main façade, given that, he aimed
to keep the original structure while at the
same time concoct something completely
original. He therefore created plaster models that he sculpted with his own hands until
achieving the shapes required and then personally oversaw the positioning of the ceramic plaques and *trencadís* work from Passeig de Gràcia. The result is a combination of
surprising shapes and intense colours that
exude a pleasant sensation of movement. As
Gaudí was such a great observer of nature,
he combined materials such as stone, glass,
ceramic work and iron, in such a way that
when the sun shone on the façade, a poetic
and warm play of light and shadow would be
evoked. As with other works by the architect, the façade of Casa Batlló has been in-
terpreted in many different ways. It has
been likened to the Mediterranean ocean or
the mountain of Montserrat. Others
have gone so far as to say that it is an
allegory to carnival time. Then
there are those who only refer to it
as *the house of bones*, for the
bonelike hollows and columns on
the rostrum. However, without a
doubt, one of the closest interpretations is the one that com-
pares the façade with Claude
Monet's paintings of the water
lilies in a pond, a clear precedent of an early case of
sculptural Impressionism.

Rostrum column

The main façade
An evocative manifestation of colour and light

Casa Batlló's main façade stands out from the neighbouring properties as an exceptional and surprising work of art. This façade, unique and unparalleled, is fruit of a perfect concoction of elements and materials. Panes that depict flowers, stones that appear bones, mask-like balconies and roof tiles that resemble a reptile's scales, indicate the overwhelming imagination of its creator: Antoni Gaudí.

An undulating cloak

When remodelling the building, Gaudí opted for, amongst other things, to modify its composite lines. The main façade was subject to a new design that hardly allowed for any trace of the previous property, only conserving the original position of its windows. Gaudí worked on various plaster models until he obtained the wavy forms he sought for the façade. The result is a curving canvas measuring 14.5 metres wide by 32 metres high and divided into three distinct parts: a stone base, a central area decorated with ceramic work and coloured glass and a roof formed by colourful scale-like roof tiles.

Sketch by Antoni Gaudí
In one of the first sketches, the architect covered the original façade with a model of roof where the tower is centrally positioned and the balconies and columns are similar to those designed for one of his other projects: Casa Calvet.

22
WINDOWS
are on the main façade of the house, three being on the main floor and the rest throughout the other floors.

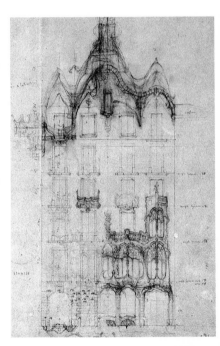

Back to its former glory
Due to the deterioration of some areas on the façade, in August 2000 another restoration was carried out. In order to get it back to its former splendour, the stone and ceramic work was cleaned and loose, broken *trencadís* work was fixed.

Material and colour

On the façade, Gaudí planned great contrasts of shapes, colours, textures and terminations. He combined different materials making the most of the plasticity and expressivity of each one: polished stone for the rostrum, glass on the walls, glazed ceramic work on the roof and cast iron on the balconies.

Vents
Small slats situated at the foot of the windows allow for ventilation.

4,80 m

32
METRES
HIGH

ROOF TERRACE

ATTIC

4TH FLOOR

3RD FLOOR

2ND FLOOR

1ST FLOOR

MAIN FLOOR

GROUND FLOOR

Façade
It is divided into three horizontal sections of different shape and material. The lower part is executed in stone, the central part is symmetrical with numerous hollows and lastly there is a ceramic, tiled roof.

1

The roof
The coloured roof tiles of scale-like form are like a reptile's skin.

The iron supports
Situated on either side of the upper balcony, they are used to haul furniture up to the flats by means of a pulley system.

4

The rostrum
Its curved lines spread out and wrap around the main floor's exterior.

3

DOORS
originally led into the house's vestibule, the shop and the car park.

The rostrum

Fruit of a complex and hazardous construction, the rostrum was erected as a key element in the façade's identity.

Rhythmic stone

When designing Casa Batlló's rostrum, Gaudí decided to integrate the entrances on the ground floor, the main floor windows and the openings on the first floor into just one sole element. Made entirely from Montjuïc sandstone, the rostrum has five openings of curving form, closed by coloured glass windows and divided by slim bone-like columns. In order to construct it,

Gaudí thought up a hazardous system that consisted of demolishing the lower part of the old façade and propping up the rest of it with precarious, wooden supports. This operation would lead to four days of anguish for the contractor Josep Bayó, who feared the façade would collapse. In order to carry out the sculpting of the stone, Gaudí created a plaster model that was used as a guide.

8 COLUMNS
Of bone-like structure are found on the rostrum windows.

2

1

The frieze drainage system
Gaudí's curving forms worked perfectly in order to drain away the rainwater.

The stained glass windows
Leaded and of lively colour, they were carried out by the Barcelona based Pelegrí Workshop.

The façade in construction, 1905. During the remodelling of the façade, a structure made from rudimentary wooden planks was used as scaffolding.

Column made from Montjuïc stone

The stone-masonry
The stonemasons sculpted the rostrum's stone as if it were a giant sculpture.

Soft forms
The rostrum's stonemasonry seems to spill out and advance like volcanic lava.

14,5 METRES
is the width of the rostrum that corresponds with the rest of the building.

LOCATION

Vegetable decoration
The rostrum has various vegetable motifs, which seem to sprout out from the stone just like plants.

Upper part
The rostrum stretches out to the sides of the first floor reaching a height of 10 metres.

Wooden windows

The rostrum and its interpretations

During this time, the façade caused quite an impact. Soon, many names were put forward in order to define it in respect to its characteristics. Due to the shape of the rostrum's windows it was dubbed the *house of yawns*, although it would become more widely known as the *house of bones*, for the shape of the stone columns between the windows.

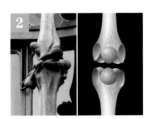

The bones. The shape and the join of the rostrum columns are very similar to human joints.

NOTE
ORGANIC FORMS

The unique shape of the upper part of the rostrum has also been likened to an enormous bat.

CASA BATLLÓ
ANTONI GAUDÍ

Decoration

Gaudí used fragments of glass and ceramic work to achieve a façade overflowing with joy.

Recycling pioneer
Gaudí used the house's broken glass and scrap tiles to adorn it.

The decoration

In order to achieve the undulating shape he sought, Gaudí instructed that some parts of the outer façade wall be carved away, managing, in this way, to create an effect of gentle movement. Later on, the façade was covered over with lime mortar, over which pieces of broken coloured glass were applied, donated by the Pelegrí Workshop, along with the Mallorcan ceramic plaques specially manufactured for the house. From the pavement of Passeig de Gràcia, Gaudí personally directed the labourers where to position these pieces, instructing them how they had to put them in order to make up groups of red, green or blue tones, and thus obtain the desired effect.

The plaques
They are of varying size and are handcrafted.

The manufacture process
The pieces were made of clay and then fired. Once fired, the colour, based on natural oxides, was then applied to them and they were then returned to the kiln to harden the varnish.

330
PLAQUES
is the approximate quantity distributed throughout the main façade.

Glazed finish

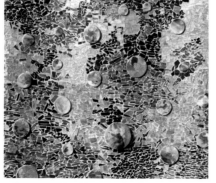

Detail. The striking colours of the glasswork.

?

WHAT IS TRENCADÍS?
It is a technique consisting of applying irregular fragments of ceramic work or other materials to cover a surface area. It was popular amongst modernist architects.

Monet's water lilies. The composition of the façade reminds of Claude Monet's water lily paintings.

Montjuïc stone
It is the material that was used in the construction of the rostrum, bestowing it with its characteristic, sandy hue.

LOCATION

They are
all different
colours

Towards abstract art

Preceding the trend for abstract art, Antoni Gaudí creates an original and fascinating work of art on the main façade of Casa Batlló. The architect knew how to adequately combine shapes and colours stemming from a correct choice of materials. Like so, he employed the assembly technique, collage, *trencadís*, and used blocks of colour, organic surfaces and shapes that generated movement, which in their totality lent the house a strong personality and set a precedent for the future artistic vanguards of the 20th century.

Undulations
Like a great ocean, the façade gently curves and seems to toss like waves.

180
METRES SQUARE
is the approximate surface area of the façade of Casa Batlló that is decorated in *trencadís*.

Hand
painted

Antoni
Gaudí

The Greeks, didn't hesitate to paint their temples, because colour instils life and we can not underrate this element to inject it in our works..."

NOTE
PLAQUE SIZE

Gaudí knew how to make the most of industrial techniques in order to standardise the ceramic circles into four different sizes and used craftsmanship so the colour would vary in all pieces.

Big Ø 35 cm	**Medium** Ø 27 cm	**Small** Ø 21 cm	**Mini** Ø 15 cm

01. Soft forms. The rostrum on the façade is sculpted as if it were a great sculpture. **02, 03 and 04.** Endings. Gaudí decorated the façade with numerous ornamental elements. **05. Melting stone.** As if it were an explosion of unusual shapes, the masonry on the rostrum and the ground floor have protrusions like a great melting rock. **06. The rostrum.** The window columns are like bones. **07. Ventilation.** Ever searching for functionalism for the elements, in the lower part of the rostrum windows, Gaudí put ventilation vents. **08. Sculpture.** In the centre of the terraces on the first floor is a sculpted element with vegetable motifs.

The balconies

Blending in perfectly with the façade arrangement, the balconies and terraces are just a part of Gaudí's creative universe.

The balustrades
They are fixed to the walls by means of two anchors, projecting out without touching the stone balcony floor.

9
BALCONIES
are on the façade, spreading out amongst the second and top floor.

4
TERRACES
These are positioned above the rostrum: two on the first floor and two on the second

The balconies and terraces

The main façade has nine balconies and four terraces, which are distributed throughout its extension. For the balconies, Gaudí designed narrow stone slabs and he positioned, on the lower part, a carving in the shape of a seashell. The balustrades, made from one piece of wrought iron, were copied from plaster models created by the architect in his workshop in Sagrada Familia. These balustrades follow the same concept used in other parts of the house: the higher up they are the smaller their hollows. For the terraces, situated above the rostrum, Gaudí designed bone-shaped balusters in gleaming, white marble from Carrara.

The shell. Gaudí linked the balconies with the sea, lending them a shell-like shape in their lower section.

Decoration
On the organically shaped terraces, the stone masonry reminds of growing plants, leaves and wild flowers.

The skull
The curved shapes, the hollows and the colour of the balcony railings are like the upper part of a human corpse.

1983
THE BALUSTRADES
are restored and their original colour recuperated, after having been painted dark grey for more than 30 years.

LOCATION

Pieces of wrought iron
To ward off rust, they were painted with lead carbonate, which gives them an ivory colour.

The iron railing
The gaps in the balustrades are closed with gilded iron sheets held by rivets.

Interpretations
Many are the lucubrations generated by the house. Without searching too far, the balconies can be compared to Venetian masks, the colour of the *trencadís* and the shape of the roof to confetti or a harlequin's hat, possibly paying homage to carnival. Yet the interpretation that carries the most weight is the one that associates the balconies with the corpses of those killed by the dragon, which was later slain by Saint George, Patron Saint of Catalonia.

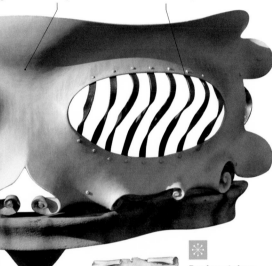

Stone base carved in the shape of a shell

Parchment shape
The irregular profile of the balustrades is similar to ripped and creased parchment paper.

Terraces above the rostrum. They possess balustrades with balusters made from white marble from Carrara.

NOTE
THE FLOWER-SHAPED BALCONY

As with all of Gaudí's creations that were inspired by the formal rules of nature, the small attic balcony has a wrought iron balustrade in the shape of a tulip or artichoke bulb.

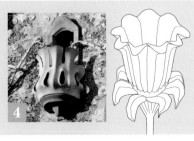

Double balustrade. All the balustrades are similar but there is one that is bigger that has three hollows.

The roof

Similar to an animal, the roof on the house is one of Antoni Gaudí's most inspired works.

The tiles
Made of ceramic work, they were specially made for the house by Sebastiá Ribó's workshop in Barcelona.

The roof and the tower

Gaudí designed an undulating surface, decorated with scale-like tiles and glazed ceramic work in shades of red, blue and green, to crown the façade and act as attic roof. On the edge of this area, he positioned some colourful spherical pieces combined with semi-circular mouldings that look like an animal's spine. As crowning piece, Gaudí planned a bulbous shaped tower, which was made in Mallorca, topped with a cross pointing towards the cardinal points.

Sentry walk. There is a narrow walkway on the lower part of the roof, like on a medieval castle.

Vertebras
At the start of the roof, Gaudí positioned a series of large-sized ceramic pieces that slot in place.
This arrangement, which architectonically represents the beginning of the roof, could symbolise an animal's long and sinuous vertebral column.

Four-armed cross

 NOTE
THE FOUR-ARMED CROSS

Gaudí topped many of his works with four-armed crosses made from varying material. Casa Batlló's is made of glazed ceramic work.

Park Güell   **Bellesguard**   **Finca Miralles**

The edge. The architect decorated the roof with helmet-shaped ceramic pieces.

> " The endings of the buildings with rickety elements, for example crosses, weathervanes, etc, are real caricatures, they're like the bald man who's got just one sole hair on his crown..."

Antoni Gaudí

Ceramic tiles

The gap
Some theories associate the hole with the rough geographical topography of the mountain of Montserrat.

600
TILES
is the approximate sum covering Casa Batlló's roof, forming a great ceramic blanket that crowns the façade.

Saint George and the dragon

Many associate Casa Batlló's main façade with the most famous episode in the life of the Patron Saint of Catalonia, Saint George (*Sant Jordi*). The undulating shape and the composition of the scale-like roof could be the mythical dragon's form. The bone-shaped columns and the balcony rails are similar to corpses and might refer to the mortalities caused by the beast. The death of the dragon may be represented by the four-armed cross, which would recall the victorious sword of Saint George, which, according to the legend, was stabbed into the beast's side leading to the fatal wound whose blood tinges this section of the roof red.

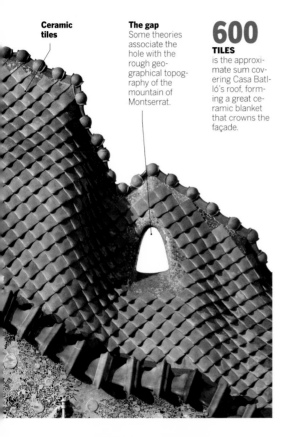

The message
High up in the tower, Gaudí put the anagrams of the Holy Family: IHS for Jesus, M for Mary, which is crowned by the ducal crown and JHP for Joseph.

Garlic bulb
The bulging shape of the tower seems to be inspired by a garlic bulb.

The tower. Crowned by a four-armed cross, it has a cylindrical base and a staircase within.

The rear façade

Gaudí planned undulating terraces, which together with vibrant colours caused a gentle feeling of movement.

The other façade

The rear façade, facing the block courtyard, shares the same undulation of the main façade but is a little more accentuated. Horizontally organized, superimposed, continuous terraces that meander inwards and outwards, follow the sinuous lines of the entire house in which Gaudí installed generous windows. Covered with iron railings, the balustrades add to a greater openness, allowing light to filter through. The façade is topped with an attic, which is like a colourful and detailed hat.

ATTIC

4TH FLOOR

3RD FLOOR

2ND FLOOR

1ST FLOOR

MAIN FLOOR

The balustrades. They are formed by panels of metal railings that cover the entire terrace.

Close up of the attic's balustrade
The triangular element is a symbol of the origin and of certain types of triads of knowledge.

Access to the terrace
On the rear façade is access to the terrace of the Batlló family residence.

LOCATION

52
WINDOWS
on the rear façade and spread throughout the five floors of residences.

Railings
Handcrafted in wrought iron and metallic grilles, they follow the curving shapes of the lucarnes.

Terraces
The façade has a long terrace on each storey.

The Batlló family apartment
A terrace, for the owner's exclusive use, can be accessed from the dining room.

Geometric shapes. Detail of the *trencadís* on the attic roof.

The decoration

The fact that this part of the Casa Batlló is facing the block courtyard didn't mean that it would merit any less of Gaudí's attention, for whom, every detail needed the closest of attention. Beautifully decorated and following the aesthetic line of the main façade, this façade combines a cheerful and colourful *trencadís* with floral and natural motifs that together with the abstract and geometrical motifs allow for a strong composite unity, characteristic of the maturity reached by the architect.

NOTE
**NATURALIST
*TRENCADÍS***

Gaudí used *trencadís* in many of his works in different ways. On the rear façade of Casa Batlló he designed floral motifs of ingenious design along with abstract and imaginative geometric motifs.

01. The oval. It planned as a termination for the rear façade. **02. Individual balcony.** The attic has a balcony facing Passeig de Gràcia. **03. Big balcony.** Only one flat has one balcony, similar in structure to the ones on the lower floors but much larger. **04. Joseph's anagram.** Carried out in ceramic work, it makes up the arrangement of three anagrams, where Jesus and Mary are represented. **05. Roof.** It tops the main façade and is one of the house's most representative elements. **06. Detail.** On the rear façade, Gaudí created avant-garde shapes. **07. Tower.** It has incrusted metal medallions. **08. Natural shapes.** On the rear façade, nature's shapes are depicted.

04

The house's vestibule. This area is decorated with blue ceramic work in relief.

THE ENTRANCEWAYS

An adaptable and evocative entrance

Gaudí designs a fluid connection between the outside and the different areas within the building.

With the renovation of Casa Batlló, Gaudí redistributes and widens areas in the former building, while planning a practical and dynamic entranceway, where different areas are connected in a fluid way. The architect set out the ground floor in order to create three very different areas: the access zone to the residences, the shop zone and the car park zone. Responding to these necessities, he designed three independent doorways: the main entrance door was made of iron and glass while the other two were made from solid oak, all perfectly blending in with the main façade by the use of stone columns. Once inside the house, a vestibule directs the movement of its inhabitants and connects with the owner's private vestibule and also with the communal staircase, which leads up to

the rented apartments. Seeking maximum functionalism, the architect widened the central patio well in order to supply this area of the house with more natural light and ventilation. Apart from the staircase, the lift was also in the patio well and on the walls were windows, lucarnes and skylights that would provide sufficient light to the apartments. All in all, all of these areas decorated with volumetric and tiled blue ceramic pieces, recreate some thought-provoking and fascinating areas inspired by the depths of the ocean.

Bannister rail

The entrance floor

Gaudí radically changes the ground plan of the former property

Gaudí enlarges and reorganizes the former rooms on this floor, giving them a new use. Thus, a wide space is created for the parking area and another for the shop, used today for other purposes. Remaining loyal to his ideas, he totally transforms the central patio well and designs the entrance to the building by means of three doorways leading into different areas on the ground floor: the house, the shop and the parking area.

The layout

During the renovation work, Gaudí redesigned the entranceways of the former property placing the entrance of the house at the far end of the façade, the parking area at the other end, and the middle area for the shop. More than 60% of the floor is reserved for the shop and the parking area; while the rest is occupied by the general vestibule and the private one, the porter's lodge, the lumber-rooms and the central patio well where the lift and neighbours' staircase are located. But without a doubt, one of the greatest innovations on this floor was to put separate entrances for the owners and tenants.

735
METRES SQUARE
is the total area taken up by the entranceway floor in the renovation carried out by Gaudí. It originally measured 500 metres square.

2

Column and beam
Of riveted iron, it gently undulates like seaweed.

3

Batlló family vestibule
The owners had a private vestibule that was accessed by means of a wide doorway located in the general vestibule.

!

The entranceway floor
The plan shows Gaudí's original project, according to what was planned during the time of the house's renovation.

Metal door
Leads through to the private vestibule of the Batlló family.

3

4

5

2

1

Vestibule

Area destined for shop

Access to parking area

1

The entranceway
Painted the same colour as the balconies, the house's doorway is made of twisting, wrought iron bars.

COMMERCIAL AREA
The space for shops was used by the Lumière photography shop, then by the cinema producer Pathé Frères and years later, in 1942, by the Syra Gallery.

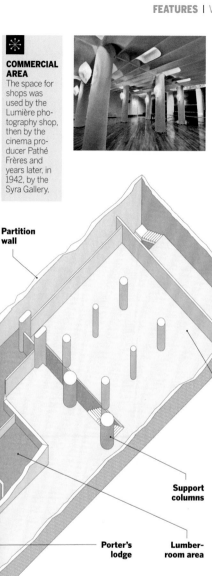

Partition wall

Rear façade

Porter's lodge

Support columns

Lumber-room area

Parking area

Stairway
It connects the basement with the main floor's back terrace.

The old parking area today
In the mid nineties this area was renovated and was transformed into a meeting and convention room.

3
DOORS
The main façade has three doors: one that leads into the house's vestibule and the other two originally belonged to the shop and parking area.

The organization of space
The central patio well vertically cuts through the house, which the flats are organized around, allowing for better ventilation and light.

The doors
Originally, the doors belonging to the shop and the parking area were made of solid wood and were opened and closed by means of a folding device. As time went on, with the shop changing owners, the doors were changed until, in 1992, as part of a big restoration, a glass and iron door was hung in the former parking area's entrance and was similar to the house's entranceway.

Central patio well. This area was devised to supply both light and ventilation to all the apartments.

Neighbours' staircase. The tenants reached their dwellings by means of a communal staircase.

The vestibule

Gaudí designs a reception area where different artistic recourses combine, resulting in the creation of an evocative space.

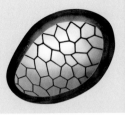

The organizer

Once inside the house, the general vestibule, of gentle shape and bluish tones, organizes and directs the traffic flow up to the different residences in the building by means of different staircases, a private one for the owners and another which is used by the tenants. Of rectangular ground plan, this cavern-like space with curved ceilings is home to the porter's lodge, and some lumber-rooms and leads directly up to the private hall of the flat on the main floor. Moreover, the Batlló family's waiting staff also used the neighbours' staircase.

On to the street. The general vestibule is the means of communication between the outside and the inside.

4

The skylight
Echoing the forms throughout the entire house, it is of oval shape and made of oak and glass.

2

Porter's lodge
The porter's lodge is situated next to the main flat's private vestibule.

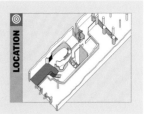

LOCATION

3

The lumber-rooms. Designed with curved lines and carved wooden doors, they are located opposite the porter's lodge and are used for storage of cleaning and maintenance things.

The doorbell panel
Situated next to the porter's lodge, the device is of modernist genre with curved, soft shapes.

Decoration

Gaudí wanted to integrate ceramic work, marble, iron and wood into just one area. He therefore used, on the lower part of the walls, volumetric ceramic pieces, positioned at an angle of 45 degrees, where grey was combined with a light blue colour, whilst the use of stuccowork was preferred higher up, which aesthetically joins the ceiling by means of drawings that resemble *trencadís*. Moreover, he used marble for the floor and wood and iron for the openings.

***Trencadís* painting.** Drawings that imitate *trencadís* work cover the plastered walls of the entire vestibule.

Materials. The decoration is a blend of different applied arts.

NOTE
THE DOUBLE DOOR OF THE PRIVATE VESTIBULE

The main floor's private vestibule can be reached from the general vestibule by first passing through an iron door, similar in shape to the exterior entrance, and then a second door made of wood and glass.

1

Ceramic work. The mosaic work of the walls alternates flat tiles with ceramic pieces in relief and volume.

The central patio well

With the renovation, this space was enlarged to ensure that light and air reached every floor in the building.

Decorated ventilation
Gaudí made the most of the tiled areas on the walls in order to include ventilation systems.

The heart of the house

Gaudí designs a central patio well which the interior of Casa Batlló revolves around and, which moreover, vertically cuts through the building, uniting every floor, from the basement to the terrace. A skylight located on the attic floor covers the well and enables light to pervade this rectangular space, which measures 13 metres long by 4 metres wide by 26 metres high. This luminous and airy patio well is the chief means of reaching the flats higher up, as it contains the lift and communal staircase.

The lift
Placed in the hollow of the neighbours' staircase, Gaudí provided all floors with a lift.

54
METRES SQUARE
is the approximate surface area that the central patio well has, after the enlargement of 1904.

Back terrace

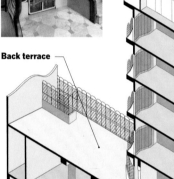

Function
The cross section shows the importance that the central patio well had on the design of the house.

 NOTE
THE CENTRAL PATIO WELL WINDOWS

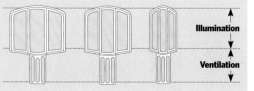

For the interior patio well, Gaudí designed windows that had a double use: their higher section was to provide light while their lower part was for ventilation.

Illumination

Ventilation

Private vestibule

Access
The patio well and the neighbours' staircase are accessed from the vestibule.

15.010
TILES
make up the decoration, in different shades of blue on the walls of Casa Batlló's central patio well.

In search of light
On the walls are numerous openings so that light can reach each and every corner of the building.

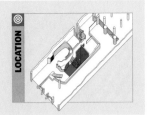

LOCATION

The skylight
Crowning the interior patio well is a large, transparent, glass skylight.

32
WINDOWS
of different size but of similar design are found in the house's central patio well.

2

The staircase and landings. In order to obtain light, the architect designed misted glass walls that flanked the landings on the neighbours' staircase.

3

The patio well terraces
To let in more natural light, terraces were put on the main floor on the first and second floor residences.

The importance of light
Gaudí completely renovated the central patio well so that all areas would receive adequate illumination. He devised different systems to carry out this function: he installed various lucarnes on the walls that open out like mouths in order to receive zenithal light and he designed internal terraces on the lower floors of the house and put up glass walls on the staircase landings, which allowed the passing of light. Moreover, larger windows are installed in the lower interior rooms on the bottom floors as they receive less light and smaller windows are installed higher up.

1

Vestibule

Main entrance

The central patio well

The architect set out to achieve a homogenous bluish light found in the depths of the ocean.

Colour and material

When it came to designing the central patio well, the architect was inspired by the depths of the ocean, which he considered synthesized three-dimensional space and the movement of life. In order to give an organic feel, Gaudí combined different shades of blue within the central patio well, by means of relief tiles or volumetric ceramic work that decorated the door and window frames. In order that illumination in this area was equal at different heights, the walls were decorated with ceramic tiles whose shade of blue would correspond to their position, with the darker ones nearer the skylight and the lighter ones positioned lower down.

The patio well
It provides light and ventilation to the flats by different systems.

The skylight
It is made of a structure made from metal profiles of catenary arch shape.

The landing
Thanks to the glass profiles the staircase has well-lit landings.

Sea effect on the glass

Patio well terrace. It has railings made from metallic mesh.

The rail ending
It has curved, spiralling forms resembling aquatic plants moved by ocean currents.

The banister
The rails that are situated in between the profiles of the staircase landings are wooden and gently undulate.

LOCATION

The basement

Gaudí enlarged this area

The basement was originally intended for different communal uses and also housed the private lumber-rooms of the Batlló family. With Gaudí's intervention, the floor area was doubled, a boiler was installed along with coalbunkers and numerous entranceways were created. Then when it was required for a new purpose, this space was renovated in 1995 and a generous multi-purpose room was created in order to hold social and cultural events.

The service area

When Gaudí planned Casa Batlló, he designed the basement as a service area where the *machineroom* of the building was located, housing the hot water tank, the coal bunkers and various lumber-rooms, which he enlarged by adding a back part onto the original space. The architect provided this floor with many entrances that linked it with the rest of the house: the basement could be accessed by descending a stairway that went around the lift, by an internal staircase descending from the main floor, or by the stair from the back terrace.

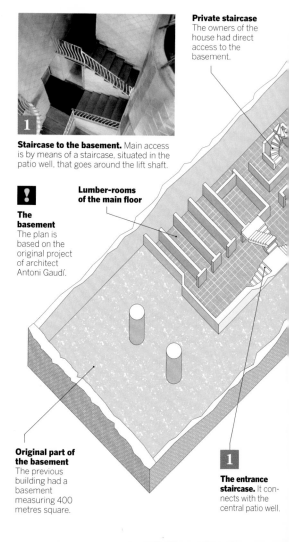

Private staircase
The owners of the house had direct access to the basement.

Staircase to the basement. Main access is by means of a staircase, situated in the patio well, that goes around the lift shaft.

!

The basement
The plan is based on the original project of architect Antoni Gaudí.

Lumber-rooms of the main floor

Original part of the basement
The previous building had a basement measuring 400 metres square.

1

The entrance staircase. It connects with the central patio well.

Lucarne. In order that light reaches the basement floor, Gaudí devised some attractive skylights.

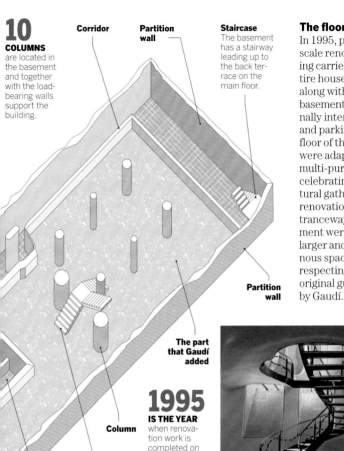

10
COLUMNS
are located in the basement and together with the load-bearing walls support the building.

Corridor

Partition wall

Staircase
The basement has a stairway leading up to the back terrace on the main floor.

Partition wall

The part that Gaudí added

1995
IS THE YEAR
when renovation work is completed on the basement. From this date on, the basement is used as a function or convention room.

Column

Coalbunkers

Staircase to the ground floor

The floor's new use

In 1995, part of the large-scale renovation work being carried out on the entire house was finished, along with work on the basement, the area originally intended for the shop and parking, and the first floor of the house, which were adapted to be used as multi-purpose rooms for celebrating social and cultural gatherings. During renovation work, the entranceways to the basement were improved and larger and more diaphanous spaces were created respecting, at all time, the original guidelines set out by Gaudí.

The new staircase. During renovation work, between 1989 and 1995, a stair was built leading down to the basement, in the space originally destined for the shop.

 NOTE
THE CAVE IN THE BASEMENT

During the enlargement of the basement, Gaudí discovered an old natural grotto that he decided to preserve. Apparently this cave was used as a cold room in the old farmhouse that had existed before the construction of the building in 1875.

The basement. Nowadays, it hosts many social events.

THE CERAMIC PIECES OF THE CENTRAL PATIO WELL

Casa Batlló holds numerous examples of applied arts, typical of the Modernist movement, such as the ceramic tiles that decorate the central patio well.

Gaudí's ceramic work
The architect designed all the ceramic pieces of the house.

SPECIAL PIECES

Gaudí entrusted the potter Sebastià Ribó with the creation of his designs for the central patio well and the vestibule. The latter made a series of matching pieces that adapted to the shapes of the door and window frames, and other pieces that alternated with the tiles on the walls.

Window frames. The pieces are combined and adapted to the patio well windows and doors.

Shape
The ceramic pieces are finished off in such a way that they seem to be eroded.

20 × 20 centimetres
is the size of the volumetric ceramic pieces of the central patio well.

Manufacture
The clay is pressed and fired twice, the last time to fix the colour.

Marine design relief

The colours. Different shades of blue are applied when creating these ceramic pieces.

In the depths
Gaudí used volumetric ceramic tiles in different shades of blue to decorate the central patio well, which gradually recreate the ocean depths.

26
METRES
is the approximate height that the central patio well reaches at its highest point.

600
METRES SQUARE
is the surface area of the decorated tiled walls on the central patio well.

Bend piece

Bend piece

Square piece

Square piece

Angle piece

Termination piece

Curved piece

Bend piece

Straight piece

Straight piece

COLOUR

In order to achieve a more homogenous light on every floor, Gaudí used a minimum of 5 shades of blue on the ceramic pieces of the central patio well, reserving the lighter, whiter shades for nearer the floor and the darker tiles for higher up.

1
Dark

2
Medium dark

3
Medium

4
Medium light

5
Light

01. The landings. Wide and luminous, they face the interior patio well. **02. The lift door.** Harmoniously combines iron, wood and glass. **03. The railing.** Made of iron rods, it is found on the inside balconies of the patio. **04. Organic shapes.** The union of different elements creates curved and gentle forms. **05. Patio well.** Source of light and ventilation for the interior rooms of the house, it is completely decorated with ceramic work. **06. Detail.** The ceramic work adapts to the patio's shapes. **07. The skylight.** An iron and glass structure allows light to come in and prevents rain from entering. **08. Ending.** Close up of ironwork.

05

The main room ceiling. The great whirlpool subtly blends in with the oak doors.

THE APARTMENTS

Functionalism and poetry

The aesthetic lends itself to the different spaces and rooms that make up Casa Batlló.

Gaudí devised Casa Batlló as a whole, without distinctions between its interior and exterior parts: the interior spaces evolve by means of curving and undulating forms that gently combine with the exterior, without abrupt differences between the façade and the inside of the building. In his overall conception of the work, the architect didn't consider aestheticism to be any more important than functionalism when putting his ideas into practise. Therefore, the entranceways, the relationship between spaces, illumination and ventilation were treated with the utmost functional meticulousness while at the same time turned into attractive spaces. During the alteration of the building, Gaudí completely renovated the main floor, where the Batlló family would live, by designing furniture and décor

in consonance with the rest of the house. In the other apartments he only carried out some minor alterations without touching their original layout. Different entranceways were created: the landlords had their own private staircase and a lift, which was also used by the tenants, who also had a communal staircase. The different elements making up the house are a blend of numerous skills such as ceramic work, glasswork, wrought iron, sculpture or cabinetmaking and combined together make the building a clear exponent of modernist art.

Stained glass window

The main floor

Gaudí completely renovates the apartment

With an area doubling that of the other flats, the Batlló family residence possesses numerous rooms along with a private terrace at the rear façade. The layout of the previous flat was completed altered in the renovation work carried out by Gaudí, leading to the creation of a series of cosy, bright, spacious areas that could be adequately adapted to the different functions of the house.

The Batlló's apartment

Measuring almost 400 metres square, it was the largest residence in the building. In the renovation work carried out to enhance the quality of light and space, Gaudí transformed the partition walls into undulating walls and designed the décor and furniture. The main entrance was reached by means of a private staircase that started in the private vestibule, next to the lift, which climbed up to a landing. The neighbours' staircase was used by servants as a secondary entrance.

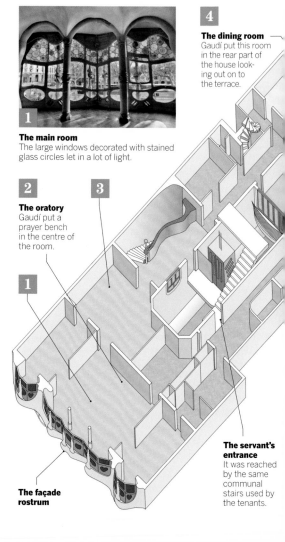

4

The dining room
Gaudí put this room in the rear part of the house looking out on to the terrace.

The main room
The large windows decorated with stained glass circles let in a lot of light.

1

2

3

The oratory
Gaudí put a prayer bench in the centre of the room.

1

The servant's entrance
It was reached by the same communal stairs used by the tenants.

2

The private vestibule. A staircase, which is like an animal's spine, goes up to the main floor.

The façade rostrum

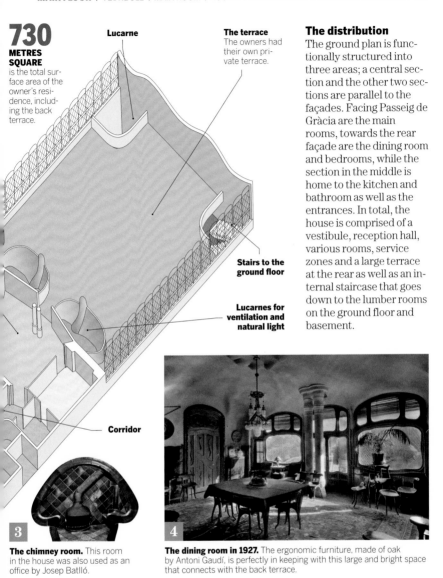

730
METRES SQUARE
is the total surface area of the owner's residence, including the back terrace.

Lucarne

The terrace
The owners had their own private terrace.

Stairs to the ground floor

Lucarnes for ventilation and natural light

Corridor

The distribution
The ground plan is functionally structured into three areas; a central section and the other two sections are parallel to the façades. Facing Passeig de Gràcia are the main rooms, towards the rear façade are the dining room and bedrooms, while the section in the middle is home to the kitchen and bathroom as well as the entrances. In total, the house is comprised of a vestibule, reception hall, various rooms, service zones and a large terrace at the rear as well as an internal staircase that goes down to the lumber rooms on the ground floor and basement.

The chimney room. This room in the house was also used as an office by Josep Batlló.

The dining room in 1927. The ergonomic furniture, made of oak by Antoni Gaudí, is perfectly in keeping with this large and bright space that connects with the back terrace.

CHRONOLOGY
100 YEARS OF CASA BATLLÓ

1906
The Batlló family move in
When work finishes on the building the owners take up residence.

1940
The children inherit it. Following the death of Josep Batlló in 1934 and Amalia Godó in 1940.

1954
Iberia Seguros **purchase it**
The insurance company purchase it in order to set up office.

1993
The company *Chupa Chups* **purchase it**
And it becomes property of the Bernat family.

The private vestibule

Gaudí paid special attention to the details of this private entrance, generating a room of organic appearance.

Close-up of the stairs
On the banister pole, metallic ribbons entwine around a crystal ball.

A special entrance

Gaudí planned a very special area that would lead up to the Batlló family's apartment. Entering from the general vestibule, a door made of iron grilles and another door, which is made of wood, go through to the landlords' private vestibule that is connected, by means of a great wooden staircase, to the reception hall on the main floor. Of organic shape, this space, which has the feature of not having any edges, generates a very fluid, flowing space where walls and ceilings merge into one. The function of the vestibule is quite simple: that the visitor can enter the house from the same entrance on the ground floor.

1

Organic skylight. Gaudí creates light-shades of circular form.

2

The vertebras
The lateral terminations of the staircase, carved from wood, are like the vertebras of the spinal column, maybe inspired by a large animal.

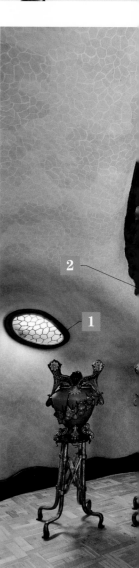

2

1

Private vestibule. As soon as they crossed the general vestibule, the Batlló family could go directly to their residence by passing through their own private vestibule that was designed by Gaudí as an organic, cave-like space.

Access from the lift

The banister rail
Gaudí designed a winding, sinuous, wooden banister that was intricately handcrafted.

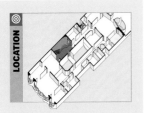

LOCATION

The staircase
With attractive, organic forms, it is made of wood and connects the ground floor vestibule with the hall on the main floor.

3

Decoration
The wall is stuccoed and painted in a series of greys imitating a large *trencadís*.

4

Door to the Batlló family's lumber-room

27
STEPS
make up the staircase, from the lower to the upper part of the vestibule.

4,40
METRES
is the drop from the top of the staircase between the private vestibule and the hall on the main floor.

The apartment hallway. It is reached by the private staircase and is the threshold of the main flat.

The staircase
In the private vestibule, the architect planned a great, carved oak staircase that would lead straight up to the main apartment. On its steps, Gaudí designed a series of decorative endings, echoing the vertebras of an animal's spine, which according to some interpretations could be the tail of the dragon depicted on the façade. As a finishing touch to the staircase there is a long, handcrafted banister that starts off wrapped around a metal pole that is decorated with a crystal ball supported by spiralling ribbons.

The main room

The architect designs a very spacious and bright functional area, with numerous decorative elements.

Handle
Even the smallest of details were considered in order to create a scene inspired by nature.

The grand room

The main room is made up of three connected spaces that face the main façade. In the central and most important space, nature's forms materialise from a whirlpool on the ceiling that circles the light, runs along the curved walls and forms three arches that delimit the rostrum window. A special guillotine style opening system was created for this window, which when opened is frameless and diaphanous.

The columns
A close-up of one of the two stone column's capitals found in the central room.

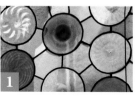

Stained glass on main window

NOTE
THE ROOM'S ORATORY

In the room, there was a piece of oratory furniture with doors that, on closing, hid an altar and an altarpiece that is now in the Sagrada Familia crypt.

105
METRES SQUARE
is the total surface area generated by joining the central room with the two on either side.

The side rooms
The spaces located on either side of the main room can also be closed off and used as independent areas.

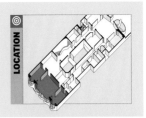

LOCATION

Functional space

Gaudí designed an ingenious door system for the main area in the flat that, according to the owners' different necessities meant that the central room could be made bigger, connecting it to the side rooms by means of large, oak doors with coloured, stained glass. They folded back, like an accordion, creating a unique space, diaphanous and luminous thanks to the rostrum's windowpanes that took up the entire length of the façade.

Ceiling. The main room's undulating ceiling swirls as if it were a whirlpool.

Oak door

2

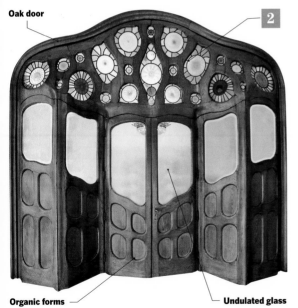

Organic forms

Undulated glass

Carved wood. Sinuous, curved and spiralling forms decorate some of the doors.

2

The stained glass
Gaudí uses different materials on the oak doors such as stained glass.

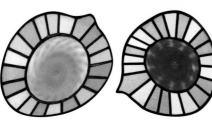

The floor
The parquet designed by Gaudí is inspired by geometric shapes.

01. The main room. In 1927, the Batlló family house had a very elegant and classic décor. 02. Handle. The door accessories designed by Gaudí, possess the same modernist essence throughout the house. 03. Lucarne. Found in the private vestibule, it is like a tortoise shell. 04. Detail. In Casa Batlló all the wooden elements are a delicate example of cabinetmaking. 05. Folding screen door. Located in the main room, the door has undulating shapes and combines glass and wood. 06. The staircase. Situated in the private vestibule it has organic and evocative forms. 07. Ventilation. Gaudí gave the rostrum windows numerous openings for ventilation.

The rooms in the house

The Batlló family had spacious areas at their disposal to carry out the different requirements of the home.

The tiles
The tiles designed by Gaudí for Casa Batlló wasn't produced in sufficient time, so it was later used in La Pedrera.

The fireplace room. The recess holds the hearth and its mushroom-shaped seating.

Functional areas

Out of all the different rooms in the apartment, what particularly stands out is the fireplace room, linking the hall with the main rooms and used, originally, as an office. With walls decorated in gold leaf, this room has a recess in the wall made of heat-resistant material, where the fireplace and benches that Gaudí designed are incorporated, inspired by the seating found in traditional Catalan houses, *escó*, which symbolised family union.

The openings
Gaudí devised the openings as original pieces of carpentry made especially for the hollow spaces.

20
AREAS
made up the main residence, including rooms and service zones.

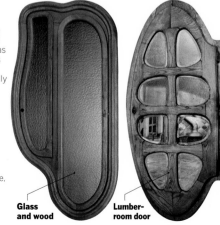

Glass and wood

Lumber-room door

Lighting
Antoni Gaudí developed different systems in order that all areas would be provided with sufficient illumination.

30
DOORS
with different designs, are those that the architect devised for the Batlló family's flat.

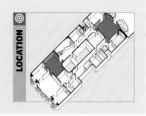
LOCATION

The dining room

Antoni Gaudí put this bright and welcoming room in the rear part of the house, next to the kitchen. Measuring 25 metres square, it boasts undulating walls and has large windows looking out on to the back terrace. The architect chose oak for the design of the furniture and doors, a material that he considered faithful to his ideas. Crowning the dining room, on the ceiling, he positioned an element that looks like droplets of water.

The dining room. Diaphanous and bright, its large windows look out on the terrace.

The column
Gaudí was inspired by the *Patio de los Leones* in the Alhambra in Granada, but its shape seems to be deteriorating and eroding.

Decorative painted *trencadís*

Service room
Originally, one room was used as a sewing room.

Access. An internal staircase goes down to the ground floor and basement.

The back terrace

Reserved for the private use of the main floor, Gaudí devised a spacious patio terrace in the rear part of the house.

A place to be enjoyed

The Batlló family had a private back terrace, measuring 230 metres square, which could be reached by means of a small bridge that, flanked by railings and three lucarnes, connected with the dining room. In the back part of the patio, on one side there is a staircase going down to the ground floor and basement, and on the other side is a large lucarne. As decoration, Gaudí applied *trencadís* to the walls in the shape of circular, ceramic plaques, similar to those on the main façade.

The terrace
It is located at the rear part of the house, over the ground floor parking area planned and constructed during the renovation of the house that was carried out between 1904 and 1906.

230
METRES SQUARE
is the total surface area of the back patio terrace that takes up the entire breadth of the building.

The railings
They were handcrafted and made of iron mesh and bars, topped off with twisted pieces.

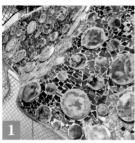

Lucarnes. These oval hollows allow for the illumination of different areas of the basement.

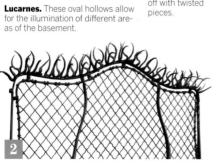

Gaudí's design
The architect designed all the elements of the patio, from the iron railings to the lucarnes decorated with *trencadís* work.

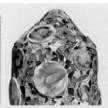

Ceramic circles
In some parts of the patio *trencadís* was alternated with ceramic circles, which are similar to those on the main façade.

LOCATION

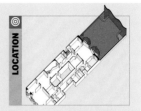

The terrace exit
Main access to the terrace is through an oak and glass door, protected by an iron grille, which connects it with the dining room on the main floor.

Skylight
The patio provides many ways for natural light to filter down below.

45.110

CERAMIC PIECES
is the approximate quantity that the present patio paving has.

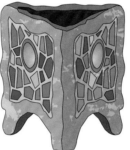

The flowerpots. Designed by Gaudí, they are decorated with coloured *trencadís* and have a triangular base.

The paving

The present borders of the patio terrace floor are no longer the originals due to deterioration and subsequent replacement. The paving carried out by Gaudí was hydraulic, mosaic work recuperated from the previous building. Under the architect's guidance, the labourers positioned the different pieces of ceramic work in a random way, generating a *trencadís* of abstract drawings.

Stairway
It links the rooms found in the rear part of the ground floor and basement.

NOTE
CERAMIC DECORATION

On the lower part of the patio a large, decorative element was put up and used as a flower bed, decorated with ceramic circles and glass *trencadís* of different shades of green, blue and red.

Ceramic

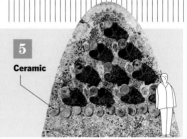

The rented apartments
Eight flats would be rented out

Gaudí didn't modify the rented apartments of the former building structurally, but redistributed all the rooms in order that sufficient light and ventilation would be obtained from the façades and central patio well. On four storeys, the apartments have all the comforts and modern devices that were possible for the era whilst achieving comfortable and harmonious spaces.

Organization of the apartments

Gaudí renovates some of the rented flats without altering their original structure. The four floors of rented properties can be reached by using the neighbours' staircase or the lift. Each floor is home to two dwellings that measure approximately 200 metres square. The eight residences are laid out in the same way: around the central patio is each service zone, with the bathrooms, kitchen and other rooms while the bedrooms, dining rooms and main rooms are next to the façades and receive sunshine in the morning and then at the rear in the afternoon.

8
RENTED FLATS are distributed throughout the four floors, all with the same internal organization and accessed by the neighbours' staircase, landings and lift.

Handle
Gaudí designed the sinuous handles and brasswork on the doors and windows.

The patio window
This opening is designed with a double function: the upper part provides light and the lower part is for ventilation.

Patio well and ventilation

Main rooms

Present day use. Some of these flats today are used as administration offices and for celebrations of private events, whilst two flats still have tenants.

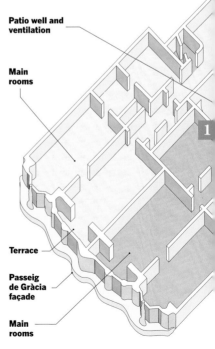

Terrace

Passeig de Gràcia façade

Main rooms

THE CIVIL WAR
During the Spanish conflict, a hundred people entered Casa Batlló causing, along with the passage of time, damage in the building.

Washing lines
The tenant's sunny terraces were ideal for hanging out the washing.

Rear terrace
The rented flats had a long, wide terrace at the rear.

A house of residences

As with many of his works, Gaudí doted the rented flats with period comforts. These dwellings were very well equipped with luxurious touches such as hot running water in the bathrooms, central heating and electric lighting. Moreover, they had laundry rooms and lumber-rooms located in the attic. At present, some tenants still reside in the rented flats in Casa Batlló.

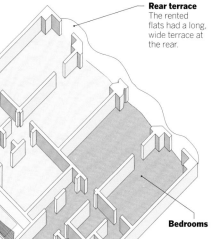

Bedrooms

Service zone

Ventilation for service rooms

Corridor

Letter that identifies the property

1906
THE FIRST TENANTS moved into Casa Batlló the same year that the Batlló's took up residence.

Look-out iron grille in door

3
The doors
On them are the letters "b" to "i", given that the letter "a" was reserved for the main floor.

Four floors for rent
Each one of the floors was divided into 2 equal flats, measuring 200 metres square, which looked out on to the two façades.

THE WOOD USED IN GAUDÍ'S DESIGNS

Polished oak was used by Antoni Gaudí in the design of the furniture, doors and windows to achieve a harmonious flow throughout Casa Batlló.

CARPENTRY

The door and window frames adapted to the curved hollows in the partition walls. Their organic appearance was emphasized with stained glass and wood carving, forming swirls and geometric lines.

150

DOORS
is the approximate total number of wooden doors inside Casa Batlló.

1

Fireplace room

THE FURNITURE

Gaudí designed the dining room furniture in varnished oak. The architect wanted the seats to easily adapt to the human form and thought about making a specific seat for each sex, although only one model was carried out in the end.

4

The chair
The wings of the chair-back are sunken in so that the chair can be easily moved around.

 Three-seater bench
Gaudí designed a three-seater seat in the style of a wooden sofa, whose size was accord with the space taken up.

2 Dining room

3 Hall door

Carved detail

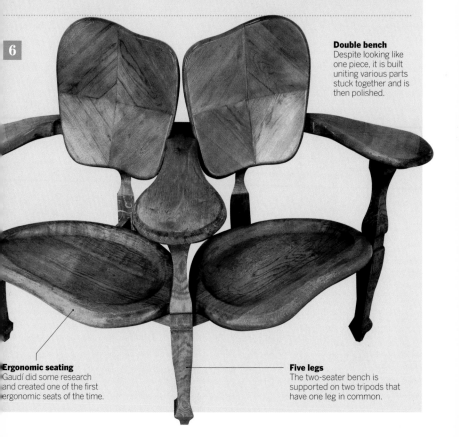

6

Double bench
Despite looking like one piece, it is built uniting various parts stuck together and is then polished.

Ergonomic seating
Gaudí did some research and created one of the first ergonomic seats of the time.

Five legs
The two-seater bench is supported on two tripods that have one leg in common.

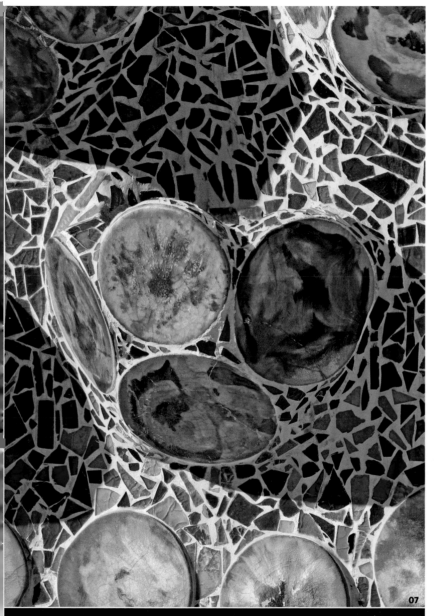

07

01. Chimney. In Josep Batlló's former office is an imaginative fireplace, constructed with fireproof brick. **02. Windows.** For better illumination and ventilation, Gaudí planned large windows for the dining room. **03. Railings.** In the rear terrace are security elements whose shapes resemble wild plants. **04. Double column.** Decorated with painted *trencadís*, it is located in the dining room. **05. Cabinetmaking.** The dining room doors are carved with attractive shapes. **06. Detail.** On the dining room ceiling is a circular piece with twelve protrusions that seem to be drops of water. **07. Ceramic sculpture.** Of large size, it is placed at the end of the rear terrace.

06

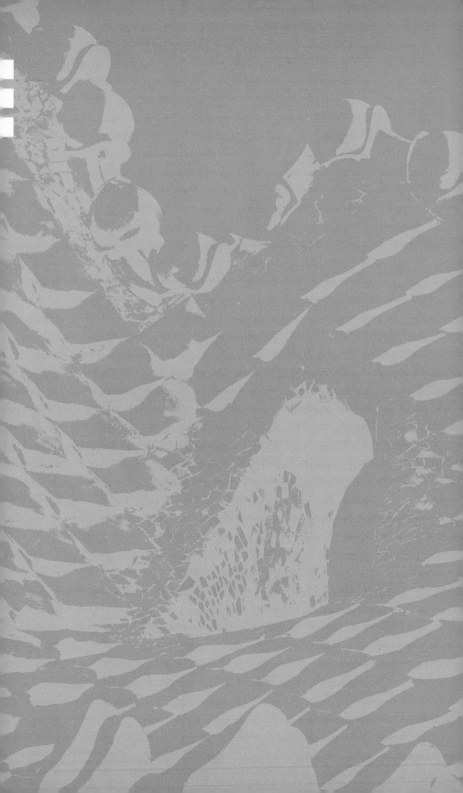

The staircase. It climbs from the attic floor up to the roof terrace.

THE ATTIC

The house's crown

Gaudí knew how to combine aestheticism and functionalism on the last floor of the house, generating a unique space.

The architect tackles the last floor of the house, the attic, as the building's crowning piece, in the expressive, artistic sense as well as the functional, in such a way that this floor is endowed with its own architectonic system and original forms, on the interior as well as the exterior. It is an independent construction in respect to the lower floors; the structure of the apartments is totally different to that of the attic and this is due overall to the fact that they are spaces that are devised for completely different uses. From the functional point of view, Gaudí plans the attic as protection chamber for the building and it is also used as service zone. He constructs it by using a series of catenary arches, solely built with brickwork, which are plastered over and support the ceiling

vaults, which the roof terrace rests on. This simple but ingenious structural device, which the architect applied in various projects such as the Teresian College and later on in La Pedrera, generates large, flowing, continuous spaces of great, evocative power that seem to take their inspiration from the rib cage of a large animal, which has subsequently lead to different interpretations comparing the attic to the inside of the dragon that is represented on the Gaudían Casa Batlló's rooftop.

Balcony. The attic has an exit looking out on to the main façade.

The attic

To crown the building, Gaudí devises an ingenious solution

The expressive forms of the attic arches are just another example of Gaudí's ability to combine the functional with the aesthetic. This thermal chamber takes its inspiration from nature: the parabolic vaults and two spiralling staircases, along with the carefully considered lighting, create an area similar to a large cave, while at the same time remind of the thorax of an enormous animal.

The thermal regulator

Gaudí designs the attic as protection chamber to shield the building from brusque changes in temperature. It is a thermal regulator inspired by the typical Catalan loft found in ancestral homes. This final floor of the house, which can only be accessed by the neighbours' staircase, was used as service area, housing the laundry rooms, washing lines and some lumber-rooms. Another smaller attic can be accessed from the terrace on the main façade, which is in the higher part of the roof and contained the house's water tank.

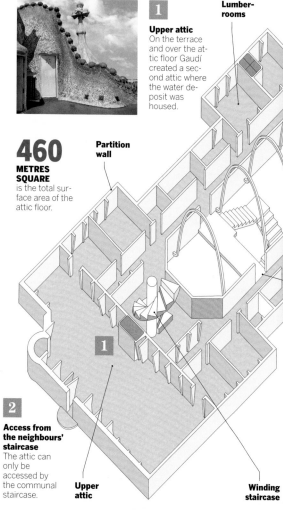

1

Upper attic
On the terrace and over the attic floor Gaudí created a second attic where the water deposit was housed.

Lumber-rooms

460
METRES SQUARE
is the total surface area of the attic floor.

Partition wall

Upper attic

Winding staircase

2

Access from the neighbours' staircase
The attic can only be accessed by the communal staircase.

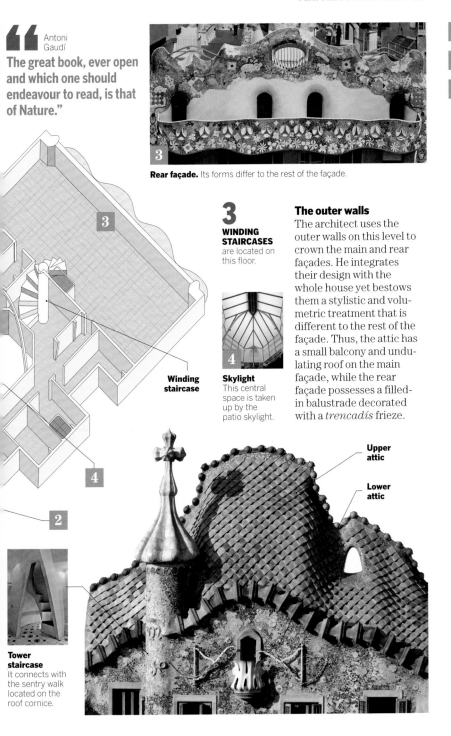

> ❝ Antoni Gaudí
>
> **The great book, ever open and which one should endeavour to read, is that of Nature."**

Rear façade. Its forms differ to the rest of the façade.

3

WINDING STAIRCASES are located on this floor.

Skylight
This central space is taken up by the patio skylight.

Winding staircase

The outer walls

The architect uses the outer walls on this level to crown the main and rear façades. He integrates their design with the whole house yet bestows them a stylistic and volumetric treatment that is different to the rest of the façade. Thus, the attic has a small balcony and undulating roof on the main façade, while the rear façade possesses a filled-in balustrade decorated with a *trencadís* frieze.

Upper attic

Lower attic

Tower staircase
It connects with the sentry walk located on the roof cornice.

An organic structure

The arches devised by Gaudí for the structure of the attic generate a large cavernous chamber of great expressiveness.

The plan view

The attic has neither the same structure nor the same architectonic organization as the rest of the house as this part of the building responds to functional criterions that differ to those of an apartment. With this in mind, the architect constructs the attic using a self-supporting system, whose vaults are supported by means of a series of catenary arches, built solely from Catalan brick, placed on their sides and then plastered over. This type of construction has the advantage of not requiring columns or support partitions, which means that the floor can be a diaphanous, flowing area, permitting freedom of movement. Gaudí used this arch system not only for these advantages but also for its simple construction.

Series of arches
Many rows of bricks make up each one of the catenary arches, which positioned one after the other create a resistant structure and allow for a characteristic, diaphanous space.

Catenary arch

Plasterwork finish

13
ARCHES are used to make up the structure of the widest section of the attic, on which the upper attic rests.

The lumber-rooms. Gaudí created many spaces on this floor to store the junk accumulated by the tenants.

The corridor. It goes around the central patio well and is used to access the different areas in the attic.

Light slats. Gaudí breaks and moves the wall to create ventilation and illumination slats.

Brick
Gaudí built the catenary arch system with ordinary brickwork, a hardy and inexpensive solution.

Organic inspiration
The series of arches in the attic might draw their inspiration from the thorax of an animal, like a whale, or possibly the hull structure of an old, wooden boat.

2004
THE RENO-VATION
of the attic means it can be visited along with the roof terrace.

WHAT IS A CATENARY ARCH?
It is a supporting structure of parabolic shape that is created by hanging a chain from both ends.

Geometry
Gaudí used geometry as his base in order to plan some elements such as staircases.

The stairs

The attic has three winding staircases, two of which connect with the roof terrace. Despite their scant decoration, they have a great evocative power thanks to the geometry of their shapes, inspired by elements from nature such as the sinuous shape of the inside of a snail shell, one of Gaudí's preferred forms. By means of the third staircase, located in the interior of the tower on the façade and smaller than the rest, the narrow sentry walkway on the roof can be accessed.

NOTE
THE ATTIC'S PRESENT DAY USE

In the year 1983, following a thorough renovation, a small museum was inaugurated in the attic area. In the year 2004, the loft was renovated once again and at present the entire floor can be visited, where holograms and other exhibition elements recreate the figure of Antoni Gaudí. The upper attic can also be visited.

The stairs. Gaudí put two winding staircases to connect the attic with the terrace.

GAUDÍ'S ATTIC ARCHES

In the house's attic, the architect developed an ingenious, architectonic solution, freeing the floor from partition walls and generating a resistant and expressive structure.

Roof tiles

Upper attic
Antoni Gaudí designed this space to hold the water tank.

Gaudí's arches

The architect was particularly fond of catenary arches as structural elements. He named them balanced arches because their shape, like a chain hung from its two ends and viewed upside down, allowed loads to be equally distributed, transforming the arch into a resistant structure that didn't require other support elements that Romanesque and Gothic arches needed. Moreover, the material was brick, which meant that construction was simple and inexpensive.

Catenary arch

The structure
By putting one catenary arch after the other Gaudí creates a very resistant structure that easily adapts to the floor's configuration.

Ceramic tiles

Façade tower

Upper attic

Façade balcony

Lower attic

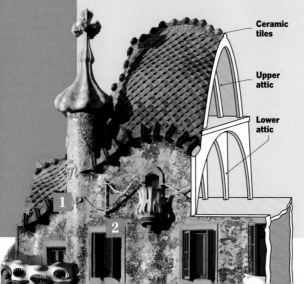

1

2

Domènech. The famous Modernist architect also used these types of archways in his projects.

OTHER WORKS

Palau Güell
In this previous work, Gaudí had already started using the catenary arches as a structure in different areas of the building.

La Pedrera
Constructed after Casa Batlló, Gaudí put 270 arches of varying width and height in the attic, generating a large, flowing space.

Floor of the upper attic

> Antoni Gaudí
>
> **In the execution of areas, geometry does not complicate the construction but actually simplifies it."**

Catenary arch

+60 ARCHES
were used by Gaudí in the construction of the attic.

Sentry walk

Floor

THE ARCHES

A Romanesque arch

B Gothic arch

C Gaudí's arch

A new archway
Thanks to its shape, the catenary arch is self-supporting, allowing for greater height without the need for buttresses that Romanesque or Gothic archways required.

01

02

03

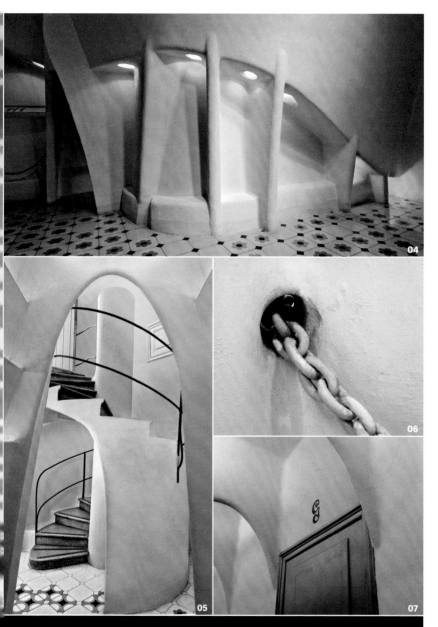

01. The arches. The series of catenary arches creates a flowing and continuous space. **02. Laundry rooms.** The attic was used as a service area and was home to the laundry rooms. **03. Lumber rooms.** Each one of the apartments had their own junk room identified by the same letter of the apartment. **04. Structure.** The resistant archway structure designed by Gaudí for the house appears to be inspired by a large animal's ribcage. **05. Winding staircase.** There are two and they allow for easy access to the roof terrace. **06. Detail.** The metal arms on the façade used as a pulley system for hauling up furniture to the flats, were pulled from the attic by means of two sets of chains. **07. Lumber room door.**

07

Trencadís. On the roof terrace, Gaudí created vibrant decoration by using ceramic pieces.

THE ROOF TERRACE

The creation of a universe

The aesthetic expressivity of Antoni Gaudí flows throughout the roof terrace of the house.

On Casa Batlló's roof terrace, Gaudí gives free rein to his imagination and uses all his creativity to transform this space, which at the start of the 20th century was hardly taken into account when planning a building, into a universe of forms, silhouettes and original textures, which transcend architecture to become sculptural pieces of great artistic merit. Apart from the poetic value of the terrace, the architect defines the functional aspect of this area of the house by organizing the floor and its elements in a logical way, and offering rational solutions for the different requirements of the area. Like so, Gaudí has two stairwells, four groups of chimneys and ventilation shafts and a small attic below the terrace, all of the latter are covered in delicately coloured *tren-cadís* work. Charged with aesthetic freedom, these sculptural pieces are constructed with curved, ductile and organic forms, inspired by the laws of nature, which the attractive and surprising universe of Antoni Gaudí revolves around. Just like other houses he built, when building Casa Batlló, the architect paid great attention to the design of its roof terrace, as he considered that this feature bestowed the building with a strong personality, similar to the hats sported by citizens of the period.

Chimney arrangement

The roof terrace

An attractive space marked out by evocative elements

The roof terrace is an example of Gaudí's artistic freedom: expressive and thought-provoking. In this area and as the house's hat, the architect arranged the elements in a functional way, organising the chimneys around the skylight and positioning the stairwells at the far ends. This is how, along with the small attic that resembles the flank of a dragon, the entire terrace has converted into a work of art.

The roof of the house

The terrace is built on top of the attic and follows the same structure by forming a large, rectangular space measuring 300 metres square, cut through in the middle by a hollow holding the central patio well skylight, and at the far ends there are four small patio wells for ventilation. The roof terrace is accessed from the attic by two winding staircases, located next to the far ends of the central patio. The terminations on the main and rear façade, acting as walls, close the terrace in.

Organic forms
The ventilation towers and smoke vents' singular bodies have vegetable or anthropomorphic-like shapes.

300
SQUARE METRES
is the total area of the surface of the Casa Batlló roof terrace.

Group of chimneys

Stairwell

Coloured trencadís

1

The attic
The upper part looking out on to the avenue is said to be the flank of the dragon slain by the Patron Saint of Catalonia, Saint George.

1

The layout of the terrace
Gaudí put the patio skylight in the middle of the floor, while the stairwells were put at either end. The upper attic was put on the main façade.

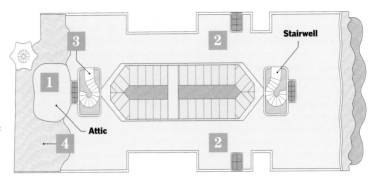

Stairwell

Attic

The elements
In order to create the attractive shapes of the elements on the terrace, Gaudí resorted to a simple system that was already in use in Gothic architecture called the bricked vault technique, which meant that he could create almost any shape with the guarantee that it was very resistant. Therefore, for the construction of the chimneys and stairwells, whole bricks or bricks cut lengthways were positioned, in order to build, with each new row, a vault with the required shape, which was then rendered over, plastered with lime mortar and decorated with colourful *trencadís* work. Moreover, Gaudí recuperated the mosaic floors of the former house and used them to pave the terrace with *trencadís* work, which has been replaced through the course of time.

Chimneys
There are four chimney arrangements: two are over the stairwells and another two on the sides of the terrace.

Stairwells
The roof terrace has two stairwells that have the same rounded shape and are decorated with *trencadís* work.

Door detail
Decorated with natural motifs, the attic door, which is located on the roof terrace, has a six-petalled flower, which has been directly fixed on to the wood.

The small window. The small opening in the attic has a parabolic shape and reminds of the *Roca Forada* of the mountain of Montserrat.

The chimneys

Gaudí turns the chimneys and ventilation shafts into sculptural elements rising from the terrace.

The flowers
The architect decorates the chimneys with elements inspired by nature, such as the *trencadís* of flowers.

Functional elements

For the smoke and ventilation vents, the architect applies all his genius and creates sculptural objects with great evocative power, without losing sight of their actual function. These elements, which originate in the kitchens and fireplaces of the apartments, along with the boiler in the basement, are grouped into four blocks. Like so, two groups, located on the stairwells, are made up of 8 chimneys, while the groups made up of 4 and 7 chimneys are located at the sides of the roof terrace floor.

Polychromatic cowl

Group of seven chimneys
Divided up into equal parts, its design has a geometric structure.

Inspired by nature
The chimney arrangements seem to grow like clusters of mushrooms.

Spherical shaped ending

Flowers

Union
Gaudí joins the chimneys higher up but separates their trunks.

Sea shapes
The sinuous forms of the *trencadís* pattern are like the waves in the ocean.

SMOKE VENT
For Gaudí, the rounded shapes of the vents meant that the smoke and hot gases couldn't swirl around and would leave more quickly and effectively.

The chimneys. The architect recreates a landscape full of fascinating shapes.

> **"Originality consists of returning to the origin, so what is original is to return to the first solutions."**
>
> Antoni Gaudí

The sphere
The original spheres on the chimneys were glass filled with coloured powder, but were then replaced in the restoration.

The cowl. The shape of the cowl helps to expel smoke.

6,10 metres

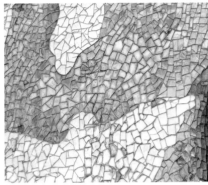

The colour. In some areas Gaudí used subtle tones.

2004
IS WHEN restoration work is finished on the terrace and chimneys, meaning they can be visited by the public.

27
CHIMNEYS were positioned by Gaudí on the building's terrace.

The decoration

In their design, the chimneys recall the popular Catalan past-time, mushroom picking, given that they seem to grow in a similar way. Their bodies are decorated with white *trencadís* combined with shades of red and blue and their shapes are like the waves in the ocean. The cowls are decorated with floral motifs and geometry of deeper shades correlating with the decoration on the rear façade.

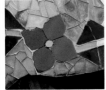

Naturalist decoration on the chimneys

THE CHIMNEYS IN GAUDÍ'S WORK

Gaudí transformed the terrace's chimneys and the ventilation shafts into grand and alluring sculptural blocks, uniting function and beauty.

Antoni Gaudí
For the architect, the terraces had to have their own character.

CASA BATLLÓ
Decorated with allusions to nature, the chimneys on this building rise up from the terrace and are organised into groups of figures, which seem to seek out light, like the mushrooms in a forest.

From above
The chimneys seen from above constitute a geometric shape.

Chimneys
Gaudí designed his chimneys originating in a trunk that seems to reach out to the sky crowned by a cowl with different decorative finishes.

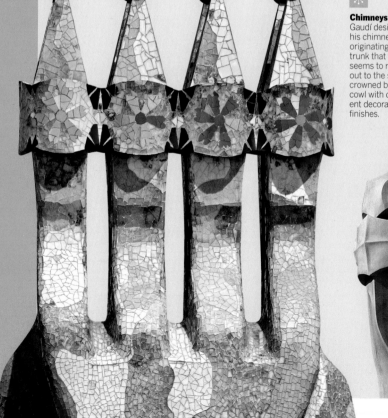

Brick

Trencadís

PALAU GÜELL
All its chimneys are different and are decorated with diverse materials such as exposed brick and coloured *trencadís*. The heads of the smoke vents, like an arrow pointing upwards, are designed with volumetric shapes and hollows.

20
CHIMNEYS
rise from the terrace of Palau Güell, which was constructed between 1886 and 1888.

The materials
Gaudí used brickwork and different types of *trencadís* in the design of his chimneys.

Interpretations
Gaudí's chimneys were subject to different interpretations as they remind of warriors, candies, mushrooms and so on.

Casa Batlló

Palau Güell

La Pedrera

Park Güell

LA PEDRERA
Gaudí planned the chimney arrangements of this house with cowls that resemble masks or the helmet in a soldier's armour.

Signs
Some chimneys are decorated with crosses and symbols related to Gaudí.

PARK GÜELL
This unique chimney on the entrance lodge of the park is decorated with *trencadís* ceramic work and has the shape of an *amanita muscaria* mushroom.

01 and 07. Groups of chimneys. With evocative shapes, the chimneys rise up like plants sprouting in search of light. **02. Stairwell.** Integrated with the smoke vents, there are two and they are the largest elements on the terrace. **03. Protection balustrade.** To carry out this function, Gaudí used an undulating wall. **04. Detail.** The chimneys are decorated with glass *trencadís* of coloured, floral motifs. **05. The dragon's flank.** The main façade's termination stands out on the roof terrace. **06. The skylight.** Located in the centre of the terrace floor, a large glass and iron skylight covers the house's central patio well.

VISUAL GUIDE CASA BATLLÓ

PUBLISHED BY
© DOS DE ARTE EDICIONES, S.L., BARCELONA, 2011

TEXTS
MANAGING DIRECTORS:
CARLOS GIORDANO AND NICOLÁS PALMISANO.
REDACTION: SOEDADE NOYA ÁLVAREZ (CHAPTER 2). VIRGINIA
LÓPEZ SÁENZ (CHAPTER 3). XAVIER BLASCO PIÑOL (CHAPTERS 4 TO 7).
ALBERTO RODRÍGUEZ AND LIONEL SOSA (CHAPTERS 1 TO 7).
© DOS DE ARTE EDICIONES, S.L., BARCELONA, 2011

TRANSLATION
AUTHOR: CERYS R. JONES.
© DOS DE ARTE EDICIONES, S.L., BARCELONA, 2011

PHOTOGRAPHS
AUTHORS: CARLOS GIORDANO AND NICOLÁS PALMISANO.

PHOTOGRAPHS OF THE CASA BATLLÓ
© CASA BATLLÓ, S.L. UNDER LICENSE OF THE PROPRIETOR.

ARCHIVE PHOTOGRAPHS
• PAGE 008 (AUTHOR: FREDERIC BALLELL).
  © ARXIU HISTÒRIC DE LA CIUTAT DE BARCELONA – ARXIU FOTOGRÀFIC.
• PAGE 034 (FONS SUGRAÑES, UNKNOWN AUTHOR).
  WITH THE COLLABORATION OF THE COL·LEGI D'ARQUITECTES DE CATALUNYA.
  © ARXIU HISTÒRIC DEL COL·LEGI D'ARQUITECTES DE CATALUNYA.
• PAGE 096.
  © BODEGAS CODORNÍU.
• PAGE 032 (ORIGINAL DRAWING OF THE FAÇADE).
  © CASA BATLLÓ, S.L.
• PAGES 004, 026, 071, 076 AND 084.
  © INSTITUT AMATLLER D'ART HISPÀNIC. ARXIU MAS.
• PAGE 006 (BARCELONA VIEW. AUTHOR: ALFRED GUESDON).
  © INSTITUT DE CULTURA DE BARCELONA, ARXIU HISTÒRIC DE LA CIUTAT.
• PAGE 074 (RELIEF OF THE HOLY FAMILY).
  © JUNTA CONSTRUCTORA DEL TEMPLE EXPIATORI DE LA SAGRADA FAMÍLIA,
  CARLOS GIORDANO AND NICOLÁS PALMISANO.

ILLUSTRATIONS
PAGES: 006 (OIL TOWER), 007 (TELEPHONE, BULB), 008 (MOTORBIKE, AUTO-
MOBILE), 009 (PROJECTOR), 010 (AIRPLANE, JOSEP BATLLÓ), 011 (TITANIC),
013 (MASK), 020, 021, 022 (PERSPECTIVE), 024, 025, 033, 041 (SKULL, FLOWER),
052 (PERSPECTIVE), 053, 056, 060 (PERSPECTIVE), 070 (PERSPECTIVE), 72, 081
(FLOWERPOT), 082 (PERSPECTIVE), 092 (PERSPECTIVE), 095, 096, 097, 108 AND 109.
AUTHORS: CARLOS GIORDANO AND NICOLÁS PALMISANO.
© DOS DE ARTE EDICIONES, S.L., BARCELONA, 2011

FOURTH EDITION, 2011

ISBN
978-84-96783-17-1

DEPÓSITO LEGAL
B-37870-2011

PRINTED IN SPAIN

DOWNLOAD
Extra Content!
www.dosdearte.com
This book contains a code that
enables you to download
an **extra chapter** from
our website

Using the code you will be
able to download extra material, visiting the "Download
zone" on our web page.

UHH2021IUJ

WITH THE COLLABORATION OF

CASA BATLLÓ
GAUDÍ
BARCELONA

Casa Batlló, S.L.
Passeig de Gràcia, 43
08007 Barcelona - Spain
Phone: +34 93 488 06 66
Fax: +34 93 488 30 90
www.casabatllo.cat

DOSDe arTe EDICIONES

www.dosdearte.com
info@dosdearte.com